The Civil Rights Act of 1964

Robert H. Mayer, *Book Editor*
Moravian College

Bonnie Szumski, *Publisher*
Scott Barbour, *Managing Editor*

OPPOSING
VIEWPOINTS® **AT ISSUE IN HISTORY**
SERIES

GREENHAVEN
PRESS®

THOMSON
—★—
GALE

San Diego • Detroit • New York • San Francisco • Cleveland
New Haven, Conn. • Waterville, Maine • London • Munich

THOMSON
————*————™
GALE

Anpam
5/05
20.00
38179000155331
9/10

LIBRARY OF CONGRESS CATALOGING-IN-PUBLICATION DATA

The Civil Rights Act of 1964 / Robert H. Mayer, book editor.
    p. cm. — (At issue in history)
  Includes bibliographical references and index.
  ISBN 0-7377-2304-1 (lib. bdg. : alk. paper) —
  ISBN 0-7377-2305-X (pbk. : alk. paper)
    1. Civil rights—United States—History. 2. United States—Civil Rights Act of
  1964. I. Mayer, Robert H., 1952– . II. Series.
  KF4749.C58 2004
  342.73'085'09—dc22   2003047288

Printed in the United States of America

Contents

Chapter 1: Politicians Debate the Civil Rights Act

Chapter 2: The American People Debate the Civil Rights Act

Chapter 3: Assessing the Act's Passage and Legacy

Foreword

Historian Robert Weiss defines history simply as "a record and interpretation of past events." Both elements—record and interpretation—are necessary, Weiss argues.

> Names, dates, places, and events are the essence of history. But historical writing is not a compendium of facts. It consists of facts placed in a sequence to tell a connected story. A work of history is not merely a story, however. It also must analyze what happened and *why*—that is, it must interpret the past for the reader.

For example, the events of December 7, 1941, that led President Franklin D. Roosevelt to call it "a date which will live in infamy" are fairly well known and straightforward. A force of Japanese planes and submarines launched a torpedo and bombing attack on American military targets in Pearl Harbor, Hawaii. The surprise assault sank five battleships, disabled or sank fourteen additional ships, and left almost twenty-four hundred American soldiers and sailors dead. On the following day, the United States formally entered World War II when Congress declared war on Japan.

These facts and consequences were almost immediately communicated to the American people who heard reports about Pearl Harbor and President Roosevelt's response on the radio. All realized that this was an important and pivotal event in American and world history. Yet the news from Pearl Harbor raised many unanswered questions. Why did Japan decide to launch such an offensive? Why were the attackers so successful in catching America by surprise? What did the attack reveal about the two nations, their people, and their leadership? What were its causes, and what were its effects? Political leaders, academic historians, and students look to learn the basic facts of historical events and to read the intepretations of these events by many different sources, both primary and secondary, in order to develop a more complete picture of the event in a historical context.

In the case of Pearl Harbor, several important questions surrounding the event remain in dispute, most notably the role of President Roosevelt. Some historians have blamed his policies for deliberately provoking Japan to attack in order to propel America into World War II; a few have gone so far as to accuse him of knowing of the impending attack but not informing others. Other historians, examining the same event, have exonerated the president of such charges, arguing that the historical evidence does not support such a theory.

The Greenhaven At Issue in History series recognizes that many important historical events have been interpreted differently and in some cases remain shrouded in controversy. Each volume features a collection of articles that focus on a topic that has sparked controversy among eyewitnesses, contemporary observers, and historians. An introductory essay sets the stage for each topic by presenting background and context. Several chapters then examine different facets of the subject at hand with readings chosen for their diversity of opinion. Each selection is preceded by a summary of the author's main points and conclusions. A bibliography is included for those students interested in pursuing further research. An annotated table of contents and thorough index help readers to quickly locate material of interest. Taken together, the contents of each of the volumes in the Greenhaven At Issue in History series will help students become more discriminating and thoughtful readers of history.

Introduction

"The problem of the twentieth century is the problem of the color line." This sentence from the pen of the great intellectual and social activist W.E.B. DuBois reflects a long sequence of events that occurred during DuBois's lifetime (1868–1963). That sequence started shortly after the Civil War with the passage of amendments to the Constitution granting fundamental rights to African Americans but continued with the subsequent stripping away of those rights. A vicious system of segregation, reinforced by violence and justified through racist ideology, was instituted instead. Following the imposition of this segregation, decades passed with little change in the status of African Americans. People living during the middle of the twentieth century might have reasonably concluded that this social and political order, this "problem of the color line," would remain intact forever. Given this long history of racial injustice, the passage of the Civil Rights Act of 1964 seems all the more miraculous.

The hope that flourished among black Americans immediately after the Civil War ended in the last decades of the nineteenth century. During those years, the system of segregation known as Jim Crow slowly developed. Still, as they had done in the past, black activists challenged the constitutionality of segregated facilities. One historic challenge came in 1892, when Homer Plessy took a seat on a New Orleans train. Plessy, an African American who could pass for white, sat in a car designated for "whites only." He promptly told the conductor that he was in fact "colored." When Plessy also refused to move to the segregated coach set aside for blacks, he was arrested and thrown into jail. Plessy's act was a calculated challenge to the Louisiana Separate Car Act of 1890, which segregated blacks and whites on passenger trains. The challenge ultimately went to the U.S. Supreme Court in the 1896 case known as *Plessy v. Ferguson*. In its ruling, the Court upheld the Louisiana law, stating that segregated train cars did not violate the Fourteenth

Amendment to the Constitution, which guaranteed equal protection to blacks, if the accommodations for each race were "equal."

The impact of this ruling was great. Previous to this time the only overt Jim Crow laws mandated segregation on trains. After the ruling, legally sanctioned segregation of facilities in many areas of southern life mushroomed. City and state laws separated African Americans from whites in theaters, train depot waiting rooms, steamboats, and hospitals, among other places. Blacks had to use specially designated water fountains and restrooms. Blacks were banned from many restaurants and hotels. Despite the separate-but-equal proviso in the *Plessy* ruling, facilities for blacks were decidedly inferior. The segregating of accommodations had evolved into a full-blown system, one designed to abase African Americans and mark them with an inferior status.

Blacks had limited means for confronting the injustice. First of all, southern politicians, by placing restrictions on voting rights, systematically deprived blacks of the ability to participate in the political process. The right to vote had been granted in the Fifteenth Amendment, passed immediately after the Civil War, and then had been taken away through a variety of means. These mechanisms included literacy tests, which required potential voters to read and interpret the state constitution, and poll taxes, which people had to pay for the "privilege" to vote. In addition, the boundaries of voting precincts were redrawn by southern state legislators so as to prevent black voters from gaining a majority, weakening the African American influence in elections. These and other methods effectively disenfranchised blacks throughout the South.

African American power was further weakened through a particularly brutal pattern of violence. Between 1882 and 1905 southern racists, supported by the silent acquiescence of other whites, lynched more than one hundred blacks a year. Meanwhile, mob violence against blacks occurred. For example, in 1898 in Wilmington, North Carolina, white gangs assaulted and killed eleven African Americans while wounding scores of others. During riots in Atlanta in 1906, white crowds roved the city freely, attacking African Americans they encountered. By some estimates, more than one hundred blacks were murdered in this outbreak. Such violence generated a fear in the African American community that made it difficult for them to speak out.

Economically, the situation was no better for blacks. Many unions for skilled workers banned blacks from membership. Because union membership was often a requirement before one could be hired, most skilled jobs were therefore closed to African Americans. Moreover, African Americans faced out-and-out discrimination from employers who refused to hire them for certain jobs. Blacks were relegated to the most grueling and menial positions. In cases where they were hired for the same jobs as whites, blacks were frequently paid less than their white counterparts. These and other factors made it impossible for African Americans to get ahead financially.

Despite a seemingly hopeless situation, from the time of slavery forward, African Americans actively fought for justice. For instance, in 1909 W.E.B. DuBois helped to form the National Association for the Advancement of Colored People (NAACP). The NAACP became the premier civil rights organization throughout the first half of the twentieth century. Organization leaders chose the courts as a primary arena for reaching goals that included an end to segregation in public education and regaining the right to vote. In addition, they launched campaigns urging Congress to pass legislation against lynching. Yet, though many persisted in the fight for civil rights and some change did occur in the first half of the twentieth century, the orchestrated effort to deny blacks a status equal to that of whites in American society seemed destined to continue.

The NAACP persisted in its efforts to challenge Jim Crow in the courts and eventually scored a major victory. In *Brown v. Board of Education*, the NAACP went before the justices of the Supreme Court and challenged the segregation of public schools. Thurgood Marshall, who at the time was the NAACP's lawyer, attacked the separate-but-equal logic that lay behind the earlier *Plessy* decision. Marshall demonstrated the material differences between black and white schools and then went on to establish the negative psychological impact of such difference on African American children. In other words, these separate-but-unequal schools taught African American children that they were inferior to white children. The Court handed down its decision in 1954. The nine justices unanimously agreed with the NAACP and overturned the *Plessy* ruling. In his written opinion, Chief Justice Earl Warren stated firmly, "Separate educational facilities are inherently unequal."

The Supreme Court's decision energized the movement to end the segregation embedded in other aspects of American society. One year after *Brown*, in Montgomery, Alabama, a black seamstress by the name of Rosa Parks refused to yield her bus seat to a white person. Her subsequent arrest sparked the first mass action of the modern civil rights movement. The black community of Montgomery pulled together and sustained a successful boycott of city buses for more than a year. Finally, the protest ended when the Supreme Court declared the segregated buses of Montgomery unconstitutional.

The boycott brought to the forefront of the public consciousness a young minister by the name of Martin Luther King Jr., who went on to organize still more protests through the newly formed Southern Christian Leadership Conference (SCLC), which he led. Then, in May 1963, the SCLC led a series of marches in Birmingham, Alabama, which was considered the most segregated city in the South. The major goal of the protest was an end to discriminatory hiring as well as segregated lunch counters, fitting rooms, and restrooms in Birmingham department stores. Bull Connor, the city's safety commissioner and an archsegregationist, ordered the use of fire hoses and police dogs to intimidate the marchers. Despite Connor's tactics, demonstrations grew even larger. Commissioner Connor arrested thousands or protesters, filling the jails of Birmingham to capacity and beyond.

Televised images of young people being attacked by police dogs and crushed against buildings by the water from fire hoses captured the sympathy of the American people, including the nation's president, John F. Kennedy. Such attention brought a great deal of pressure to bear on the leaders of Birmingham. In response, civic leaders signed an agreement acceding to some of the key demands made by the SCLC, including an end to segregated facilities in Birmingham stores and promises to hire more black clerks.

The protests in Birmingham had an important impact at the national level. Though President Kennedy had supported civil rights as a candidate, he had done little to promote civil rights during his first two years in office. One month after the Birmingham agreement was signed, President Kennedy went on national television to call for a federal civil rights bill. Though his speech sounded a note of urgency, Kennedy proceeded with caution. He expected a difficult fight in a Congress that included southerners who would argue assiduously against changing the southern way of life. Kennedy chose to introduce the bill in the House of Representatives, where he knew it would face an easier battle than in the Senate. Emanuel Celler, a liberal Democrat from New York and a strong proponent of civil rights, was chair of the House Judiciary Committee where the legislation would face its first test. Celler worked with William M. McCulloch, the ranking Republican on the committee, to pass the bill. Kennedy's hope rested on creating such a coalition of liberal Democrats and moderate Republicans. To hold that coalition together, Kennedy worked to create a bill that was substantive but not so strong that it would fail to gain the support of a majority on the floor of the House.

In the midst of deliberation over the bill, two important events occurred that served to focus attention on the need for meaningful civil rights legislation. On August 28 more than a quarter of a million people participated in the March on Washington. Along with other goals, the marchers backed Kennedy's push for a civil rights bill and called for the strongest possible legislation. The second event took place on September 15. On that day in Birmingham, white supremacists set off a bomb in the Nineteenth Street Baptist Church, which had been the staging area for many of the demonstrations that had taken place in May. People across the nation were aghast to learn that the blast killed four young girls who had been in the basement of the church.

Advocates experienced their first success on October 22, when the House Judiciary Committee voted to send the bill to the floor of the House for consideration. At this point, however, tragedy brought all congressional business to a halt. On November 22 John F. Kennedy was assassinated. Now, the future of the civil rights bill depended on the desires and priorities of the new president, Lyndon Johnson.

Supporters of the bill were uncertain of Johnson's position. The president was a southerner with a mixed track record on issues involving civil rights. Less than a week after the assassination, however, Johnson quelled any fears of civil rights proponents when he addressed both houses of Congress and stated, "First, no memorial oration or eulogy could more eloquently honor President Kennedy's memory than the earliest passage of the civil rights bill for which he fought so long."

With Johnson's support, the bill moved from the House Rules Committee to passage on the the House floor in less than two weeks. One significant change took place during the amendment process. The word *sex* was added in Title VII,

On August 28, 1963, more than 250,000 people from around the nation united for the March on Washington.

the section that sought to end discrimination in job hiring. Ironically, that change had been proposed by a conservative southern congressman, Howard W. Smith, in hopes of killing the legislation. Smith had figured there would be few in Congress who would support the notion of protecting women against job discrimination. He was wrong. When the bill came to the floor of the House, it passed 290 to 130 with strong support from both Democrats and Republicans. The vote did reflect a division between North and South. Ninety-six of the nay votes came from the South. The bill then moved on to the Senate.

In the Senate the bill faced a more formidable obstacle, the filibuster. The filibuster is a strategy unique to the Senate whereby a senator may talk for as long as he or she wishes about some pending legislation. Only if a two-thirds majority votes to end the debate—that is, invoke cloture— does the filibuster end. That means that one-third of the Senate, a minority, can block a piece of legislation. Given that the twenty-one southern senators needed only twelve more senators to block cloture, the civil rights act was in serious jeopardy. In fact, cloture was rare and had never been attained when civil rights legislation was involved.

Senator Hubert H. Humphrey, a liberal Democrat from Minnesota who was a passionate advocate for civil rights, navigated the bill on its journey through the Senate. He knew that the legislation's survival depended on garnering support from twenty-two of the thirty-three Senate Republicans in order to end the debate. Humphrey began the process of coalition building by forming a bipartisan leadership team with Thomas Kuchel, the Republican minority whip. Ultimately, however, the key to success was the backing of the Republican minority leader, Everett Dirksen. As President Johnson told Humphrey, "The bill can't pass unless you get Ev Dirksen."

Dirksen, a man known for his curly white hair and gravelly voice, did work with the Democrats to create a bill he and other Republicans could accept. Despite his involvement, Dirksen's ultimate support was not a foregone conclusion. Moderate and conservative Republicans, including Dirksen, were worried about the power over American lives the new law would give to the government. Months of backroom bargaining and compromise had to take place. As negotiations continued, southern Democrats filibustered on the Senate floor. Speeches would commonly last two hours, but some marathons went on as long as eight hours. The Senate could carry on no other business.

Senators faced pressure from the American public, which strongly favored the bill. For example, a Harris poll indicated that 70 percent of all Americans supported civil rights legislation. Adding to the pressure, clergy from many faiths lobbied senators to vote for the bill. This clerical backing provided a constituency for senators from rural and western states that did not have a significant African American population. At the same time, seminary students maintained a twenty-four-hour-a-day vigil around the Lincoln Memorial, also in support of the law. Both the lobbying and the vigil elevated the climate in which the bill was considered. Passing the civil rights act became an act of moral urgency.

Through five months of arduous deliberation, Democratic and Republican senators worked toward compromise. Dirksen, knowing that conservative Republicans would oppose the use of massive federal power to prevent employment discrimination, worked to amend the bill in order to allow states to deal with discrimination before the federal government got involved. The same was true for public accommodations. States would be permitted to end segregated facilities on their own before the federal government acted. In the end, the senators hammered out a piece of legislation that

Martin Luther King Jr. and others watch as President Lyndon Johnson signs the historic Civil Rights Act on July 2, 1964.

was acceptable to enough Republicans to end the filibuster.

The dramatic vote for cloture came on June 10. Dirksen rose on the floor of the Senate and delivered an emotional speech calling for an end to the filibuster and for passage of the legislation. Cloture passed with bipartisan support. When a vote on the bill itself occurred, it passed by a margin of seventy-three to twenty-seven. President Lyndon Johnson signed the Civil Rights Act of 1964 on July 2, making it the law of the land.

The main portions of the Civil Rights Act dealt with issues central to the lives of all Americans. The act made it illegal to deny an individual the right to vote on account of race. (This section turned out to be ineffective and was eventually strengthened through the Voting Rights Act of 1965.) It also ended segregation in public accommodations, including restaurants, motels, theaters, and sports arenas and outlawed discrimination in any program that received money from the federal government. One of the most important and controversial parts of the bill, Title VII, banned discrimination "on the basis of race, color, religion, sex" in hiring by firms with twenty-five or more employees. Finally, the new law permitted the Justice Department to more actively intervene to desegregate public schools and colleges.

With the president's signature, life was changed in significant ways for all Americans. The Civil Rights Act of 1964 ended the segregation of public facilities. It opened up new employment opportunities for African Americans and women. Overall, it led to a richer involvement in areas of life long denied to black Americans.

Four decades after the fact, most Americans accept the changes brought by the legislation and view them as obviously right. Yet it is important to realize that when the Civil Rights Act was passed, many Americans did not accept the bill's goals. Passage of a strong civil rights act was not a foregone conclusion. As the speakers in this volume attest, feelings were intense on both sides of the issue. The fervently held views of southern politicians and pundits could have easily held sway and history might have gone in a different direction. What ultimately brought the hopes of African Americans to fruition? Through careful study of the various positions presented in this volume, readers are encouraged to answer that question for themselves.

Chapter **1**

Politicians Debate the Civil Rights Act

1

Congress Must Act to Protect Civil Rights

John F. Kennedy

John F. Kennedy acted cautiously in the area of civil rights during the first two years of his presidency. Despite this desire to move slowly, demonstrations forced Kennedy's hand. In particular, there were mass protests in Birmingham, Alabama. Americans witnessed the TV footage of demonstrators attacked by police dogs and young people being viciously hosed by the Birmingham Fire Department. Those images from Birmingham moved both the young president and the nation. Martin Luther King's call for the simple right of African Americans to sit at a lunch counter or to be hired in the stores where they shopped stood in stark contrast to the brutality of the city's reaction to that call.

On June 11, 1963, President Kennedy went on national television and asked for civil rights legislation that would end the conditions that led to the Birmingham actions. He called for the desegregation of public accommodations, a renewed push to end segregation in public schools, and increased protection of African American voting rights. Excerpts from that speech are presented below. The legislation Kennedy introduced was stalled in the House when the president was assassinated in November 1963. The job of attaining passage of the law would then fall to the southern vice president, Lyndon Baines Johnson.

G ood evening my fellow citizens:
This afternoon, following a series of threats and defiant statements, the presence of Alabama National Guards-

John F. Kennedy, radio and television address to the American people, June 11, 1963.

men was required on the University of Alabama to carry out
the final and unequivocal order of the United States District
Court of the Northern District of Alabama. That order
called for the admission of two clearly qualified young Alabama residents who happened to have been born Negro.

That they were admitted peacefully on the campus is
due in good measure to the conduct of the students of the
University of Alabama, who met their responsibilities in a
constructive way.

I hope that every American, regardless of where he
lives, will stop and examine his conscience about this and
other related incidents. This Nation was founded by men
of many nations and backgrounds. It was founded on the
principle that all men are created equal, and that the rights
of every man are diminished when the rights of one man
are threatened.

Possibility in America

Today we are committed to a worldwide struggle to promote
and protect the rights of all who wish to be free. And when
Americans are sent to Viet-Nam or West Berlin [two areas
where American troops were sent in the early sixties], we do
not ask for whites only. It ought to be possible, therefore, for
American students of any color to attend any public institution they select without having to be backed up by troops.

It ought to be possible for American consumers of any
color to receive equal service in places of public accommodation, such as hotels and restaurants and theaters and retail
stores, without being forced to resort to demonstrations in
the street, and it ought to be possible for American citizens
of any color to register to vote in a free election without interference or fear of reprisal.

It ought to be possible, in short, for every American to
enjoy the privileges of being American without regard to his
race or his color. In short, every American ought to have the
right to be treated as he would wish to be treated, as one
would wish his children to be treated. But this is not the case.

The Negro baby born in America today, regardless of
the section of the Nation in which he is born, has about
one-half as much chance of completing high school as a
white baby born in the same place on the same day, one-
third as much chance of completing college, one-third as
much chance of becoming a professional man, twice as

much chance of becoming unemployed, about one-seventh as much chance of earning $10,000 a year, a life expectancy which is 7 years shorter, and the prospects of earning only half as much.

It ought to be possible . . . for every American to enjoy the privileges of being American without regard to his race or color.

This is not a sectional issue. Difficulties over segregation and discrimination exist in every city, in every State of the Union, producing in many cities a rising tide of discontent that threatens the public safety. . . .

We are confronted primarily with a moral issue. It is as old as the scriptures and is as clear as the American Constitution.

The heart of the question is whether all Americans are to be afforded equal rights and equal opportunities, whether we are going to treat our fellow Americans as we want to be treated. If an American, because his skin is dark, cannot eat

A family gathers around the television on June 11, 1963, to listen to President Kennedy as he calls for a federal civil rights bill.

lunch in a restaurant open to the public, if he cannot send his children to the best public school available, if he cannot vote for the public officials who will represent him, if, in short, he cannot enjoy the full and free life which all of us want, then who among us would be content to have the color of his skin changed and stand in his place? Who among us would then be content with the counsels of patience and delay?

One hundred years of delay have passed since President Lincoln freed the slaves, yet their heirs, their grandsons, are not fully free. They are not yet freed from the bonds of injustice. They are not yet freed from social and economic oppression. And this Nation, for all its hopes and all its boasts, will not be fully free until all its citizens are free.

One hundred years . . . have passed since President Lincoln freed the slaves, yet their heirs . . . are not fully free.

We preach freedom around the world, and we mean it, and we cherish our freedom here at home, but are we to say to the world, and much more importantly, to each other that this is the land of the free except for the Negroes; that we have no second-class citizens except Negroes; that we have no class or caste system, no ghettoes, no master race except with respect to Negroes?

Now the time has come for this Nation to fulfill its promise. The events in Birmingham and elsewhere have so increased the cries for equality that no city or State or legislative body can prudently choose to ignore them. . . .

What Congress Must Do

Next week I shall ask the Congress of the United States to act, to make a commitment it has not fully made in this century to the proposition that race has no place in American life or law. The Federal judiciary has upheld that proposition in the conduct of its affairs, including the employment of Federal personnel, the use of Federal facilities, and the sale of federally financed housing.

But there are other necessary measures which only the Congress can provide, and they must be provided at this session. The old code of equity law under which we live commands for every wrong a remedy, but in too many communities, in too many parts of the country, wrongs are inflicted on Negro citizens and there are no remedies at law. Unless the Congress acts, their only remedy is in the street.

I am, therefore, asking the Congress to enact legislation giving all Americans the right to be served in facilities which are open to the public—hotels, restaurants, theaters, retail stores, and similar establishments.

This seems to me to be an elementary right. Its denial is an arbitrary indignity that no American in 1963 should have to endure, but many do.

I have recently met with scores of business leaders urging them to take voluntary action to end this discrimination and I have been encouraged by their response, and in the last 2 weeks over 75 cities have seen progress made in desegregating these kinds of facilities. But many are unwilling to act alone, and for this reason, nationwide legislation is needed if we are to move this problem from the streets to the courts.

I am also asking the Congress to authorize the Federal Government to participate more fully in lawsuits designed to end segregation in public education. We have succeeded in persuading many districts to desegregate voluntarily. Dozens have admitted Negroes without violence. Today a Negro is attending a State-supported institution in every one of our 50 States, but the pace is very slow.

I am . . . asking the Congress to enact legislation giving all Americans the right to be served in facilities which are open to the public.

Too many Negro children entering segregated grade schools at the time of the Supreme Court's decision 9 years ago will enter segregated high schools this fall, having suffered a loss which can never be restored. The lack of an adequate education denies the Negro a chance to get a decent job.

The orderly implementation of the Supreme Court decision, therefore, cannot be left solely to those who may not have the economic resources to carry the legal action or who may be subject to harassment.

Other features will also be requested, including greater protection for the right to vote. But legislation, I repeat, cannot solve this problem alone. It must be solved in the homes of every American in every community across our country. . . .

Pushing for Equality

This is one country. It has become one country because all of us and all the people who came here had an equal chance to develop their talents.

We cannot say to 10 percent of the population that you can't have that right; that your children cannot have the chance to develop whatever talents they have; that the only way that they are going to get their rights is to go into the streets and demonstrate. I think we owe them and we owe ourselves a better country than that.

Therefore, I am asking for your help in making it easier for us to move ahead and to provide the kind of equality of treatment which we would want ourselves; to give a chance for every child to be educated to the limit of his talents.

As I have said before, not every child has an equal talent or an equal ability or an equal motivation, but they should have an equal right to develop their talent and their ability and their motivation, to make something of themselves.

We have a right to expect that the Negro community will be responsible, will uphold the law, but they have a right to expect that the law will be fair, that the Constitution will be color blind, as Justice Harlan said at the turn of the century.

This is what we are talking about and this is a matter which concerns this country and what it stands for, and in meeting it I ask the support of all our citizens.

Thank you very much.

2

Debate in the Senate Chamber

Hubert H. Humphrey and Russell Long

After wending its way through several committees, the civil rights law passed in the House of Representatives on February 10, 1964. It then moved to the Senate. Here supporters of the bill faced their toughest fight. Opponents attempted to kill the legislation through nonstop discussion on the Senate floor, a strategy called a filibuster. With debate dragging on for eighty-three legislative days, both sides had ample opportunity to present their position. Excerpts from the *Congressional Record* capture the spirit of that conversation.

The pro-bill position is conveyed by Senator Hubert H. Humphrey from the state of Minnesota. Humphrey, a strong supporter of civil rights, served in the Senate from 1948 to 1964 and led the fight for passage of the 1964 civil rights bill. Russell Long, a Louisiana senator from 1962 to 1980, argues against the bill.

In the following excerpts, taken from the debate of March 24, 1964, the senators present some of the major arguments for and against the civil rights legislation. Senator Long contends that the Title II section of the bill forcing integration of public accommodations violates businessmen's right to do with their property as they choose. Senator Humphrey counters that government frequently regulates businesses and then cites several examples. He concludes by proclaiming the law's central purpose: to end the indignity that a system of segregation imposes.

Hubert H. Humphrey and Russell Long, *Congressional Record*, 88th Congress, 2nd session, 1964.

Mr. LONG of Louisiana. The situation which developed in New Orleans recently seems to be one which we should be encouraging. Some of it was brought about by picketing and other pressures. Pressure was brought to have a national chain of hotels permit colored visitors to share the facilities of the hotels. The chains yielded to that pressure. Some of the managers thought they had a moral obligation to admit colored visitors to share their facilities. So they agreed to admit colored guests.

There are two major hotels in New Orleans, both locally owned, that did not see fit to go along with that policy. Those two hotels continue to be segregated hotels; the others accept colored guests. It may very well be that those two hotels may have better business over the short run, but over a longer period of time the other hotels may have as much business. However, in New Orleans one can go to a hotel that will accept as guests only those who are members of the Caucasian race; or he can go to a hotel—which includes the majority of the big ones—that admits all who apply, such as most hotels do in the District of Columbia.

They are required by law to accept all guests regardless of race, but I believe they do a little bootlegging on segregation in the District of Columbia, because some hotels have a higher percentage of colored guests than do others. But that, to me, would seem to be the preferable way, to leave it up to the individual businessman to decide whom he wishes to serve in his hotel. . . .

A Communist Plot

Here is a letter from Mr. and Mrs. C.E. Cornell of Garden Grove, Calif.:

Dear Senator Long: We respectfully request and urge you to oppose with all of your powers, and to vote against the presently pending civil rights legislation. We believe in basic civil rights but we are convinced that the present civil rights legislation is sponsored and backed by persons and groups who are sympathetic to communism and who want to use minority votes to insure election of so-called liberals. The Civil Rights Act of 1963 is a blueprint for total Federal regimentation and is skillfully drawn with the patent, deliberate intent to destroy all effective constitutional limitations upon the extension of Federal governmental power over individuals and the States.

Never in the history of nations governed by elected officials has the head of any state demanded the naked untrammeled power embodied in this act, except when such state was upon the verge of becoming a dictatorship. If it is enacted, the States will be little more than local governmental agencies, existing as appendages of the central Government and largely subject to its control. The legislation assumes a totally powerful National Government with unending authority to intervene in all private affairs among men, and to control and adjust property relationships in accordance with the judgment of Government personnel.

That . . . would . . . be the preferable way, to leave it up to the individual businessman to decide whom he wishes to serve in his hotel.

The Civil Rights Act of 1963, if enacted, will be the first major legal step in establishing a brutal totalitarian police state over the American people, and will delve into the intimate, personal property rights of the individual.

Yours very truly. . . .

Business Organization Argues Against the Bill

Mr. LONG. Here is an excellent letter from the National Retail Merchants Association. This is a nationwide organization, which would be confronted with the results of the bill, if enacted, in ways both direct and indirect. I should like to read this letter. It comes from the national offices in Washington, D.C. It reads:

National Retail Merchants Association,

Washington, D.C., August 14, 1963.

Hon. Russell B. Long,

U.S. Senate, Washington, D.C.

Dear Senator Long: As the Congress considers the President's proposals in the field of civil rights, we wish to report to you the results of a recent survey by the association. The National Retail Merchants Association is a voluntary association of department, specialty, and chain stores located in every State in the Union and in most communities. At the request of the Attorney General [member of President's cabinet in charge of legal issues] we asked our members to advise us what progress had been made with regard to problems relating to racial matters. The results of this survey indicated quite clearly that an overwhelming majority of our members had made substantial strides in integrating their operations.

[Mr. LONG of Louisiana. Let us keep in mind that these people are under pressure from the Attorney General and others to achieve integration.]

Several of our southern stores reported that for the past 3 years they have been hiring non-whites in selling and non-selling capacities. One of the largest stores in a nearby Southern State reported that out of 3,000 employees, 400 are Negroes and that some 60 are employed in selling and non-selling functions, with several classified as junior and senior executives. These jobs were formerly held by whites.

On the basis of our study it would seem that a Federal statute such as the one being considered dealing with public accommodations is neither needed nor advisable.

Sincerely,

John C. Hazen, *Vice President, Government.*

They are the views of the National Retail Merchants' Association. Do they want the bill? No; they are against it. They are against it—North, East, South, and West.

Mr. HUMPHREY. Mr. President, will the Senator yield?

Mr. LONG of Louisiana. I yield.

A man who owns private property does not have a complete right to use it as he wishes.

Mr. HUMPHREY. Does not the letter reveal that integration or the employment of colored persons in a retail establishment did not cause any difficulty? The organization seems to report on conditions with a great deal of enthusiasm. The fact of access to public accommodation is established by the letter. The letter reveals and demonstrates that it is a good practice to have people treated as people; to hire them on the basis of merit; to permit people who are citizens of the United States to trade and to do business in public places.

What the letter also says, in effect, is that, "Since we do this freely and voluntarily, we need no law." For those who act as the letter indicates, no law is needed; but for those who do not, some law is needed.

Mr. LONG of Louisiana. The Senator from Minnesota reads into that letter something that is not there. Of course, he has every bit as much right to read between the lines as I have to read between the lines. What the letter is saying, by the light of the Senator from Louisiana, is this: "We have been pushed by the use of all the powers at the executive level. An attempt has been made to make us integrate the stores. We have yielded to quite a bit of pressure. People have been picketing out front, saying, 'Do not buy where you cannot be hired.' So we have yielded to a considerable extent to all these pressures, to all the picketing of our stores, and to one thing and another. In doing so, we have gone a long way with you, voluntarily, to the extent that we integrated, although no law required it. However, in some respects we have been forced to do this. We think there is no case for passing a law which makes it necessary to have the Attorney General enter into the picture and impose racial quotas on us. We think we have gone far enough in cooperating with the Government and do not think the kind of law that is proposed is justified. . . ."

The Rights of Business Debated

Mr. LONG of Louisiana. The Senator from Louisiana does not believe that we ought to take the step which the Senator from Minnesota now desires to take. What the Senator from Minnesota is attempting in the bill would in effect make public property of a man's private property. That is his private business. He has a right to do business with those with whom he wishes to do business. If he thinks that his business would be hurt by integrating and going contrary to the local customs and traditions, he has a right to continue his practice. I contend that he should continue to have the right to operate his business in the way he thinks is best for him.

The average small businessman has a heavy responsibility to his own family when he makes a decision of that kind, because if he should operate his business in such a way that he would go broke, his wife and children would suffer.

Mr. HUMPHREY. The Senator from Louisiana has made a point which I know means a great deal to him about the right of a man who owns his own business to operate it. I am sure that most of us who have any background in business have pretty strong feelings on that subject.

My community of Minneapolis, Minn., is a rather modern and progressive community. It is one of the better off communities in the Nation, with high employment, high per capita income, the Minnesota Twins, the Minneapolis Symphony, the Walker Art Gallery, the Minnesota Institute of Fine Arts, the Guthrie Theatre, and an urban redevelopment center. It is a marvelous community. Nevertheless, recently in that great community there was quite an argument over what was called Sunday closing.

Passing a Federal law that the people of the South are against . . . would be a mistake. It could not be enforced.

Some States have blue laws. Some cities have what are called blue ordinances, which require that on Sunday business places must be closed. The laws were the subject of one of the big arguments in our city.

A man who owns private property does not have a complete right to use it as he wishes, because when a legislature provides that a business be closed on Sunday, it must be closed on Sunday. That is the law. Such a statute denies the owner of a business the unlimited use of his property.

I remember that the argument was made, "If I could stay open on Sunday, I could make more money. Whose business is this? It is my business. Why do you legislators tell me that I cannot remain open on Sunday?"

The difference is that the legislature told them that it was the law of the State—as it is in certain other States—that they be closed on Sunday. That is true in many areas.

Returning to the entertainment industry, the Senator can go to Chicago, and he will observe that in the city of Chicago nightclubs are open until 4 o'clock in the morning. But if he goes to the city of Minneapolis, he will observe that the latest hour a nightclub can be open during the week is 1 A.M., and Saturday the closing hour is 12 midnight.

In our part of the country one never feels better than he does on Saturday night. That is the great night of the week. But despite the fact that all of us country boys always looked forward to Saturday night as the night of the week for all the enthusiastic good living that we had wanted to have all week long, when we would go to the big city on Saturday night, the city ordinance required that at 12 o'clock sharp the nightclubs close. There sits that businessman with all the goods and goodies on his shelves. There are the customers pounding on the door, rattling silver dollars, and shaking $5 bills, saying, "I want to do business. Sell me something." The merchant is eager to make some money. The tavern keeper is anxious to sell some of his "tonic"; but the law says, "Sorry, Mr. Private Enterprise, but your business must close at 12. Sorry, Mr. Customer, the law says there shall be no business after 12."

If that is not interference with private property, I never heard of it; but it is done in the name of community interest. . . .

Mr. LONG of Louisiana. I saw the point made on TV, or I read it somewhere. I believe Roy Wilkins [head of the National Association for the Advancement of Colored People] emphasized, at the time of the [August 1963] march on Washington, that approximately one-third of the marchers were white. Those white people believed in integration. They believed in mixture. Let them mix. If someone does not wish to mix, he should not be made to mix.

My idea is that a man should have complete freedom to decide whether he wishes to mix or not. If he wishes to do so, that is all right. If he does not wish to, he does not have to. Federal compulsion one way or the other should not coerce him.

I believe there is a fifth freedom—that is, freedom of dignity.

Observing what is going on in the Southern States, I know what the majority of people down there are up against. The people and their local government officials believe it would not only not be a good law—just as the majority of Americans believed that prohibition was a bad law from its very beginning—but they believe it is evil and morally wrong. That is how they feel about it. They believe it would lead to an amalgamation of the races. They believe it would lead to a great deal of pressure for racial intermarriage, and things of that kind. They believe it is a bad idea. They feel that if they had been subject to such laws over the period of the past 200 years, the South would be like the populations in Central and Latin America, where one cannot tell one race from another. It is said that there is no color line down there. One race cannot be distinguished from another. They believe it is a mistake. They believe it is wrong.

They would like to see the colored man advance. They want to help him. They have the kindliest of feelings toward him, but they have a strong moral judgment against racial mingling to begin with. Passing a Federal law that the people of the South are against as a matter of moral judgment would be a mistake. It could not be enforced. It would make for all kinds of hard feeling, ill will, and evasion. It would tend to make the colored man believe that he has those rights but the whites will not respect them. . . .

Freedom of Dignity

Mr. HUMPHREY. Mr. President, will the Senator from Louisiana yield further?

Mr. LONG of Louisiana. I yield.

Mr. HUMPHREY. I respect the Senator's argument. I do not wish my comments here to be interpreted in any sense as in opposition to what I know to be the spirit and philosophy of the Senator from Louisiana; namely, one of aiding people to help themselves, of expanding their educational and health opportunities.

No Senator has demonstrated by his actions, his words, and his deeds a greater sense of social consciousness for the welfare of the people of the United States than has the Senator from Louisiana. I mean that in all sincerity.

We are approaching a most difficult piece of legislation, and I appreciate the restrained and thoughtful manner in which the Senator from Louisiana has argued his case.

What I see in the bill is not forced integration. What I see in the bill is statutory law that will bring into effect clearly and unmistakably the elimination of segregation, that is, public segregation, segregation imposed by State law or local ordinance or imposed against a citizen of the United States by custom.

This bill definitely does not demand "Mix the races all up." I consider the bill as providing opportunity for every citizen of the United States to enjoy the benefits of his community and his Nation.

With due respect for all Senators, after a man has worked hard to get an education in high school, and perhaps a college or technical education, and has received this blessing of enlightenment, it means more to him that he will be accepted as a desired member of the community than the fact that he exercises that acceptance.

After a man of color has received a degree from a great university, if he is to be rejected at a lunch counter, or at an ordinary drugstore because of his color, it is an insult to him.

What he needs is freedom of dignity or freedom from indignity.

I spoke at a dinner the other night called the Four Freedoms Foundation Award dinner. We remember Franklin Roosevelt's four freedoms: freedom of speech, freedom of conscience, freedom from fear, and freedom from want.

I believe there is a fifth freedom—that is, freedom of dignity.

It is not so much that the individual may want to go into every hotel, or will go into every hotel, or into every tavern, or into every restaurant. If he should want to do that as a human being, he should not have a hand put out and have someone say, "Stop. The reason you cannot come in here is the color of your skin."

A Negro has no control over the color of his skin. He did not select his color at birth. He did not select the country of his birth. But he is an American. He is a citizen.

This question boils down basically to a situation in which thousands of people are privileged to have this great education, who know the literature of our civilization and the history of our country, and who have been called upon to perform every service for their country in peace and in war but suffer indignities solely because of the color of their skin.

Such a man may be a citizen of the State of Ohio who attended Western Reserve University, a nonsegregated school, and perhaps he obtained a Ph. D. degree in engineering or in physics or in medicine. Then he travels to another part of the country, even if it is only on a mission of tourism. He is a refined gentleman. He has a good income. He has a nice family. He has a good car. He is a man of good manners. He walks up to the desk of a hotel and the clerk looks at him and says, "I am sorry; we do not take colored people here."

This man knows that there is another hotel where perhaps he can sleep. It is not sleep he wants. It is acceptance; it is respect; it is the right to refuse. No amount of sleep or food will cure the injury that the man has suffered.

That is what the bill is all about. I am not unmindful of the fact that the Senator from Louisiana has told us a number of truths tonight. I dislike some of them. However, we know there are certain facts of life, and we are realists. We know that there are customs and habits of people, which will take many generations to change.

I wish to be frank with the Senator. If we pass the bill, it will not cure all our civil rights problems. If anyone thinks it will, he is only deluding himself and perhaps attempting to delude others. We believe that this would be a legal framework in which we could hope to find means of adjudicating and moderating and setting some of the problems of human relations.

As someone has put it—this may be an extreme way of putting it—what we seek to do is to take the issue of civil rights off the streets and to put it into the legislative assembly and into the courts.

I believe that is the better way to do it. We are trying to solve the problem. It is better to do it this way than to hand the problem to people who might become violent. It is better to have respect for one another and to talk these things out and try to find means of solving the problem. I do not know whether we shall be able to do it. The Senator from Louisiana has given a great deal of his life to helping people. Anyone who thinks that the Senator from Louisiana, because he opposes the bill, is against so-called civil rights, is doing a disservice to the Senator and the Senate.

3

A Threat to Our System of Government

Barry Goldwater

For the civil rights bill to pass, some congressional Republicans needed to support it. Though bill adherents were successful in swaying many Republicans to their side, one stark exception was Arizona senator Barry Goldwater. Goldwater, an outspoken conservative, expressed concern over the power that the public accommodations and fair employment portions of the bill would place in the hands of the federal government. He argued that shifting such power from state and local governments was unconstitutional and would generate a climate in which citizens would spy on one another. On June 18, 1964, one day before passage of the civil rights bill, Goldwater expressed these views on the Senate floor. This speech is presented below.

Barry Goldwater served in the Senate for five terms, from 1952 to 1987. His tenure was interrupted by a run for the presidency in 1964, when he was soundly defeated by then-president Lyndon Johnson. Due to his stand on the civil rights act, he received little support from the African American community in his presidential bid.

There have been few, if any, occasions when the searching of my conscience and the reexamination of my views of our constitutional system have played a greater part in the determination of my vote than they have on this occasion.

I am unalterably opposed to discrimination or segregation on the basis of race, color, or creed, or on any other ba-

Barry Goldwater, address to the U.S. Senate, June 18, 1964.

sis; not only my words, but more importantly my actions through the years have repeatedly demonstrated the sincerity of my feeling in this regard.

This is fundamentally a matter of the heart. The problems of discrimination can never be cured by laws alone; but I would be the first to agree that laws can help—laws carefully considered and weighed in an atmosphere of dispassion, in the absence of political demagogery, and in the light of fundamental constitutional principles.

For example, throughout my 12 years as a member of the Senate Labor and Public Welfare Committee, I have repeatedly offered amendments to bills pertaining to labor that would end discrimination in unions, and repeatedly those amendments have been turned down by the very members of both parties who now so vociferously support the present approach to the solution of our problem. Talk is one thing, action is another, and until the Members of this body and the people of this country realize this, there will be no real solution to the problem we face.

Too Much Emotion

To be sure, a calm environment for the consideration of any law dealing with human relationships is not easily attained—emotions run high, political pressures become great, and objectivity is at a premium. Nevertheless, deliberation and calmness are indispensable to success.

It was in this context that I maintained high hopes for this current legislation—high hopes that, notwithstanding the glaring defects of the measure as it reached us from the other body and the sledge-hammer political tactics which produced it, this legislation, through the actions of what was once considered to be the greatest deliberative body on earth, would emerge in a form both effective for its lofty purposes and acceptable to all freedom-loving people.

It is with great sadness that I realize the nonfulfillment of these high hopes. My hopes were shattered when it became apparent that emotion and political pressures—not persuasion, not commonsense, not deliberation—had become the rule of the day and of the processes of this great body.

One has only to review the defeat of commonsense amendments to this bill—amendments that would in no way harm it but would, in fact, improve it—to realize that political pressure, not persuasion or commonsense, has come to rule the consideration of this measure.

I realize fully that the Federal Government has a responsibility in the field of civil rights. I supported the civil rights bills which were enacted in 1957 and 1960, and my public utterances during the debates on those measures and since reveal clearly the areas in which I feel that Federal responsibility lies and Federal legislation on this subject can be both effective and appropriate. Many of those areas are encompassed in this bill and to that extent, I favor it.

Objections to the Bill

I wish to make myself perfectly clear. The two portions of this bill to which I have constantly and consistently voiced objections, and which are of such overriding significance that they are determinative of my vote on the entire measure, are those which would embark the Federal Government on a regulatory course of action with regard to private enterprise in the area of so-called public accommodations and in the area of employment—to be more specific, titles II and VII of the bill. I find no constitutional basis for the exercise of Federal regulatory authority in either of these areas; and I believe the attempted usurpation of such power to be a grave threat to the very essence of our basic system of government; namely, that of a constitutional republic in which 50 sovereign States have reserved to themselves and to the people those powers not specifically granted to the Central or Federal Government.

If it is the wish of the American people that the Federal Government should be granted the power to regulate in these two areas and in the manner contemplated by this bill, then I say that the Constitution should be so amended by the people as to authorize such action in accordance with the procedures for amending the Constitution which that great document itself prescribes. I say further that for this great legislative body to ignore the Constitution and the fundamental concepts of our governmental system is to act in a manner which could ultimately destroy the freedom of all American citizens, including the freedoms of the very persons whose feelings and whose liberties are the major subject of this legislation.

My basic objection to this measure is, therefore, constitutional. But, in addition, I would like to point out to my colleagues in the Senate and to the people of America, regardless of their race, color, or creed, the implications involved in the enforcement of regulatory legislation of this sort. To give genuine effect to the prohibitions of this bill will require the creation of a Federal police force of mammoth proportions. It also bids fair to result in the development of an "informer" psychology in great areas of our national life—neighbors spying on neighbors, workers spying on workers, business spying on businessmen—where those who would harass their fellow citizens for selfish and narrow purposes will have ample inducement to do so. These, the Federal police force and an "informer" psychology, are the hallmarks of the police state and landmarks in the destruction of a free society.

I repeat again: I am unalterably opposed to discrimination of any sort and I believe that though the problem is fundamentally one of the heart, some law can help—but not law that embodies features like these, provisions which fly in the face of the Constitution and which require for their effective execution the creation of a police state. And so, because I am unalterably opposed to any threats to our great system of government and the loss of our God-given liberties, I shall vote "no" on this bill.

This vote will be reluctantly cast, because I had hoped to be able to vote "yea" on this measure as I have on the civil rights bills which have preceded it; but I cannot in good conscience to the oath that I took when assuming office, cast my vote in the affirmative. With the exception of titles II and VII, I could wholeheartedly support this bill; but with their inclusion, not measurably improved by the compromise version we have been working on, my vote must be "no."

If my vote is misconstrued, let it be, and let me suffer its consequences. Just let me be judged in this by the real concern I have voiced here and not by words that others may speak or by what others may say about what I think.

My concern extends beyond this single legislative moment. My concern extends beyond any single group in our society. My concern is for the entire Nation, for the freedom of all who live in it and for all who will be born into it.

It is the general welfare that must be considered now, not just the special appeals for special welfare. This is the time to attend to the liberties of all.

This is my concern. And this is where I stand.

4

Morality Dictates That the Bill Be Passed

Everett Dirksen

Proponents of the civil rights bill assiduously sought the support of Senate minority leader Everett Dirksen. As a Republican party chief, his influence could swing key votes. Liberal Democrats such as Hubert Humphrey worked closely with Dirksen, and the legislation grew into a bill the Republican senator could accept. Dirksen's agreement came just in time. A filibuster had dragged on for months. The only way to stop the filibuster was through a process called cloture, which required two-thirds of the Senate to vote to end the debate. On June 10, 1964, Everett Dirksen delivered his historic speech calling for end to the debate. It worked. With a vote of 71-29, the filibuster ended that day. Most of Dirksen's dramatic address is printed below.

Dirksen, known for his gray wavy hair and gravelly voice, was first elected to the House in 1932, where he served for sixteen years. In 1950, he was elected to the Senate from his native Illinois and served there until his death in 1969. In 1959, Senator Dirksen was picked to be minority leader for Senate Republicans. As minority leader, he was thrust into a pivotal position during consideration of this and other civil rights bills.

It is a year ago this month that the late President Kennedy sent his civil rights bill and message to the Congress. For two years, we had been chiding him about failure to act in this field. At long last, and after many conferences, it became a reality.

Everett Dirksen, address to the U.S. Senate, June 10, 1964.

After nine days of hearings before the Senate Judiciary Committee, it was referred to a subcommittee. There it languished and the administration leadership finally decided to await the House bill.

In the House it traveled an equally tortuous road. But at long last, it reached the House floor for action. It was debated for 64 hours; 155 amendments were offered; 34 were approved. On February 10, 1964, it passed the House by a vote of 290 to 130. That was a 65-percent vote.

It was messaged to the Senate on February 17 and reached the Senate calendar on February 26. The motion to take up and consider was made on March 9. That motion was debated for sixteen days and on March 26 by a vote of 67 to 17 it was adopted.

"Stronger than all the armies is an idea whose time has come."

It is now 4 months since it passed the House. It is 3½ months since it came to the Senate calendar. Three months have gone by since the motion to consider was made. We have acted on one intervening motion to send the bill back to the Judiciary Committee and a vote on the jury trial amendment. That has been the extent of our action.

Sharp opinions have developed. Incredible allegations have been made. Extreme views have been asserted. The mail volume has been heavy. The bill has provoked many long-distance telephone calls, many of them late at night or in the small hours of the morning. There has been unrestrained criticism about motives. Thousands of people have come to the Capitol to urge immediate action on an unchanged House bill.

For myself, I have had but one purpose and that was the enactment of a good, workable, equitable, practical bill having due regard for the progress made in the civil rights field at the state and local level. . . .

Reasons for Cloture

There are many reasons why cloture [vote calling for end to debate] should be invoked and a good civil rights measure enacted.

First. It is said that on the night he died, Victor Hugo

[nineteenth-century French author] wrote in his diary, sub-stantially this sentiment:

> Stronger than all the armies is an idea whose time has come.

The time has come for equality of opportunity in shar-ing in government, in education, and in employment. It will not be stayed or denied. It is here.

The problem began when the Constitution makers per-mitted the importation of persons [slaves] to continue for another twenty years. That problem was to generate the fury of civil strife seventy-five years later. Out of it was to come the Thirteenth Amendment ending servitude, the Fourteenth Amendment to provide equal protection of the laws and dual citizenship, the Fifteenth Amendment to pro-hibit government from abridging the right to vote.

America grows. America changes. And on the civil rights issue we must rise with the occasion.

Other factors had an impact. Two and three-quarter mil-lion young Negroes served in World Wars I, II, and Korea. Some won the Congressional Medal of Honor and the Dis-tinguished Service Cross. Today they are fathers and grand-fathers. They brought back impressions from countries where no discrimination existed. These impressions have been transmitted to children and grandchildren. Meanwhile, hundreds of thousands of colored have become teachers and professors, doctors and dentists, engineers and architects, artists and actors, musicians and technicians. They have be-come status minded. They have sensed inequality. They are prepared to make the issue. They feel that the time has come for the idea of equal opportunity. To enact the pending mea-sure by invoking cloture is imperative.

Second. Years ago, a professor who thought he had de-veloped an uncontrovertible scientific premise submitted it to his faculty associates. Quickly they picked it apart. In agony he cried out, "Is nothing eternal?" To this one of his associates replied, "Nothing is eternal except change.". . .

To my friends from the South, I would refresh you on the words of a great Georgian named Henry W. Grady [journal-ist]. On December 22, 1886, he was asked to respond to a toast to the new South at the New England society dinner. His words were dramatic and explosive. He began his toast by saying:

> There was a South of slavery and secession—that South is dead. There is a South of union and freedom—that South thank God is living, breathing, growing every hour.

America grows. America changes. And on the civil rights issue we must rise with the occasion. That calls for cloture and for the enactment of a civil rights bill.

Third. There is another reason—our covenant with the people. For many years, each political party has given major consideration to a civil rights plank in its platform. Go back and reexamine our pledges to the country as we sought the suffrage of the people and for a grant of authority to manage and direct their affairs. Were these pledges so much campaign stuff or did we mean it? Were these promises on civil rights but idle words for vote-getting purposes or were they a covenant meant to be kept? If all this was mere pretense, let us confess the sin of hypocrisy now and vow not to delude the people again. . . .

I can only say that our party found its faith in the Declaration of Independence in which a great Democrat, Jefferson by name, wrote the flaming words:

> We hold these truths to be self-evident that all men are created equal.

That has been the living faith of our party. Do we forsake this article of faith, now that equality's time has come or do we stand up for it and insure the survival of our party and its ultimate victory? There is no substitute for a basic and righteous idea. We have a duty—a firm duty—to use the instruments at hand—namely, the cloture rule—to bring about the enactment of a good civil rights bill.

A Moral Issue Whose Time Has Come

Fourth. There is another reason why we dare not temporize with the issue which is before us. It is essentially moral in character. It must be resolved. It will not go away. Its time has come. Nor is it the first time in our history that an issue with moral connotations and implications has swept away the resistance, the fulminations, the legalistic speeches, the ardent but dubious arguments, the lamentations and the thought patterns of an earlier generation and pushed forward to fruition.

More than sixty years ago came the first efforts to secure federal pure food and drug legislation. The speeches made on this floor against this intrusion of federal power sound fantastically incredible today. But it would not be stayed. Its time had come and since its enactment, it has been expanded and strengthened in nearly every Congress.

Pending before us is another moral issue.

When the first efforts were made to ban the shipment of goods in interstate commerce made with child labor, it was regarded as quite absurd. But all the trenchant editorials, the bitter speeches, the noisy onslaughts were swept aside as this limitation on the shipment of goods made with sweated child labor moved on to fulfillment. Its time had come. . . .

Ninety-five years ago [1870] came the first endeavor to remove the limitation on sex in the exercise of the franchise. The comments made in those early days sound unbelievably ludicrous. But on and on went the effort and became the Nineteenth Amendment to the Constitution. Its time had come. . . .

These are but some of the things touching closely the affairs of the people which were met with stout resistance, with shrill and strident cries of radicalism, with strained legalisms, with anguished entreaties that the foundations of the Republic were being rocked. But an inexorable moral force which operates in the domain of human affairs swept these efforts aside and today they are accepted as parts of the social, economic and political fabric of America.

Call for Cloture

Pending before us is another moral issue. Basically it deals with equality of opportunity in exercising the franchise, in securing an education, in making a livelihood, in enjoying the mantle of protection of the law. It has been a long, hard furrow and each generation must plow its share. Progress was made in 1957 and 1960. But the furrow does not end there. It requires the implementation provided by the substitute measure which is before us. And to secure that implementation requires cloture.

Let me add one thought to these observations. Today is an anniversary. It is in fact the one hundredth anniversary of the nomination of Abraham Lincoln for a second term for the presidency on the Republican ticket. Two documents became the blueprints for his life and his conduct. The first was the Declaration of Independence which proclaimed the doctrine that all men are created equal. The second was the Constitution, the preamble to which began with the words:

> We, the people . . . do ordain and establish this Constitution for the United States of America.

These were the articles of his superb and unquenchable faith. Nowhere and at no time did he more nobly reaffirm that faith than at Gettysburg 101 years ago [1863] when he spoke of "a new nation, conceived in liberty and dedicated to the proposition that all men are created equal."

It is to take us further down that road that a bill is pending before us. We have a duty to get that job done. To do it will require cloture and a limitation on debate as provided by a standing rule of the Senate which has been in being for nearly fifty years. I trust we shall not fail in that duty.

That, from a great Republican, thinking in the frame of equality of opportunity—and that is all that is involved in this bill.

To those who have charged me with doing a disservice to my party—and there have been many—I can only say that our party found its faith in the Declaration of Independence, which was penned by a great Democrat, Thomas Jefferson by name. There he wrote the great words:

> We hold these truths to be self-evident, that all men are created equal.

That has been the living faith of our party. Do we forsake this article of faith, now that the time for our decision has come?

There is no substitute for a basic ideal. We have a firm duty to use the instrument at hand; namely, the cloture rule, to bring about the enactment of a good civil rights bill.

I appeal to all senators. We are confronted with a moral issue. Today let us not be found wanting in whatever it takes by way of moral and spiritual substance to face up to the issue and to vote cloture.

Chapter 2

The American People Debate the Civil Rights Act

1

The Bill Will End Discrimination in Public Accommodations

Roy Wilkins

Roy Wilkins, executive secretary for the National Association for the Advancement of Colored People (NAACP), appeared before the Senate Commerce Committee on July 22, 1963. In his remarks, he offered support for President Kennedy's proposed civil rights legislation. Specifically, he argued for what would later become Title II of the bill, a section requiring that segregation in public accommodations be ended. Wilkins emphasized the indignity African Americans faced every day living under segregation. He described, for instance, the ordeal of family vacations where travel had to be planned around the motels and restaurants that refused service to blacks. In refuting those who argued that abolishing segregated facilities denied property rights to businessmen, Wilkins reminded the senators that the same point was made by slave owners to justify slavery. His statement before the Commerce Committee is printed below.

Founded in 1909 and still active today, the NAACP has vigorously fought for civil rights through the courts and through active lobbying for pro–civil rights legislation. Wilkins served as leader of the organization from 1955 to 1977.

The public accommodations section seeks to invoke protective legislative action in a most sensitive area where great numbers of citizens suffer daily—almost hourly—hu-

Roy Wilkins, testimony before the Committee on Commerce, U.S. Senate, July 22, 1963.

miliation and denial simply because of their skin color. These people are citizens of the United States, not merely citizens of the States wherein they reside. As such, they are entitled to the protection of the Congress of the United States against the infringement of their rights under color of any local or State law or custom.

From the time they leave their homes in the morning, . . . until they return home at night, humiliation stalks them.

As is the case with so many aspects of the vast minority rights question in our country, the tendency in debate has been to treat the complaints in a detached laboratory manner. Hypothetical questions are posed. Hairline delineations are set forth. Labyrinthine technicalities are pursued. Precedents, often bordering on the chicken versus egg level, are solemnly intoned. Expediency, usually on a rarefied political level but festooned with fine and flowing phrases, is held forth as morality or as reason, or, worse still, as "practicality."

The Daily Indignity of Segregation

The truth is that the affronts and denials that this section, if enacted, would correct are intensely human and personal. Very often they harm the physical body, but always they strike at the root of the human spirit, at the very core of human dignity.

It must be remembered that while we talk here today, while we talked last week, and while the Congress will be debating in the next weeks, Negro Americans throughout our country will be bruised in nearly every waking hour by differential treatment in, or exclusion from, public accommodations of every description. From the time they leave their homes in the morning, enroute to school or to work, to shopping or to visiting, until they return home at night, humiliation stalks them. Public transportation, eating establishments, hotels, lodginghouses, theaters and motels, arenas, stadiums, retail stores, markets, and various other places and services catering to the general public offer them either differentiated service or none at all.

For millions of Americans this is vacation time. Swarms

of families load their automobiles and trek across country. I invite the members of this committee to imagine themselves darker in color and to plan an auto trip from Norfolk, Va., to the gulf coast of Mississippi, say, to Biloxi. Or one from Terre Haute, Ind., to Charleston, S.C., or from Jacksonville, Fla., to Tyler, Tex.

How far do you drive each day? Where and under what conditions can you and your family eat? Where can they use a rest room? Can you stop driving after a reasonable day behind the wheel or must you drive until you reach a city where relatives or friends will accommodate you and yours for the night? Will your children be denied a soft drink or an ice cream cone because they are not white?

You have to pick a route; a route sometimes a little out of the way. I have known many colored people who drove from the East to California, but they always drove through Omaha, Cheyenne, and Salt Lake City, and Reno. They did not take the southern route. And if they were going to Texas, they stayed north as long as they could. They did not go down the east coast and across the South. They went across the Middle West and down the South.

Where you travel through what we might call hostile territory you take your chances. You drive and you drive and you drive. You do not stop where there is a vacancy sign out at a motel at 4 o'clock in the afternoon and rest yourself; you keep on driving until the next city or the next town where you know somebody or they know somebody who knows somebody who can take care of you.

Will your children be denied an ice cream cone because they are not white?

This is the way you plan it.

We stop in private homes in many cases.

Of course it must be understood in some areas now this problem does not present itself; I am happy to say in an increasing number of areas. But it is still a very great problem. And it is likely to be encountered even in areas which are thought to be free of it.

What do you do in the middle of Iowa, for example, in a small town? You have almost as much of a problem as if you were in a small town in, say, Alabama.

In some of the border cities you are likely to have trouble. In others, not.

How do you figure these things out? The answer is that you do not figure them out. You just live uncomfortably, from day to day.

How Can Demonstrations Be Wrong?

It must be remembered that the players in this drama of frustration and indignity are not commas or semicolons in a legislative thesis; they are people, human beings, citizens of the United States of America. This is their country. They were born here, as were their fathers and grandfathers before them, and their great-grandfathers. They have done everything for their country that has been asked of them, even to standing back and waiting patiently under pressure and persecution, for that which they should have had at the very beginning of their citizenship.

They are in a mood to wait no longer, at least not to wait patiently and silently and inactively.

They are not to be dissuaded by talk that they are "hurting their cause" through demonstrations. No one noticed their cause except to lambast or subvert it, during the years they waited for the Nation to act positively in support of the Supreme Court decision. How can a cause which has been betrayed by every possible device, beaten back in the crudest and most overt fashion and distorted in highsounding misrepresentation by the suave kinfolk of the mob—how can a cause in such condition be hurt by the crying out of those who suffer and by their determination to alter the pattern of persecution?

The Property Rights Argument

Nor are the demonstrators and their sympathizers and supporters impressed with the contention that the Congress ought not legislate in this field. It is contended that such legislation as is here proposed—that U.S. citizens be protected from humiliating racial discrimination in public places and services in their own country—is an invasion of "property rights."

It is strange to find this argument, in connection with the fortunes of this particular class of citizens, made in 1963. This was the argument of slavery time. It was argued then that if the United States were to free human slaves, it would be invading property rights. Today, 100 years later, if the United States legislates to secure non-discriminatory treatment for the descendants of the slaves, it will be invading property rights. It is ironical that a proponent of this argument should be a representative of the State of Abraham Lincoln.

What rights, gentlemen, are thus being defended? Legal human slavery is gone, but its evil heritage lives on, damaging both the descendants of the slaves and the descendants of those who owned them—or those who have identified themselves with that class. Is not the "property rights" argument but an extension of the slave ownership argument? The disclaimers would be loud and indignant if it were suggested that any Senator approved human slavery; but how fine is the line between approval of slavery and acquiescence in a major derivative of the slave system.

This was the argument of slavery time.

The answer has to be that our Nation cannot permit racial differentiation in the conduct of places of public accommodation, open to the public and with public patronage invited and solicited. While such establishments may be privately owned, they owe their life and their prosperity not to the personal friends and relatives of the proprietors, but to the American public, which includes today, as it has for generations, all kinds of Americans. The proprietors of small establishments, including tourist homes and gasoline filling stations, are no less obligated to render nondiscriminatory public service than are the proprietors of huge emporiums or hostelries.

Return to Core American Principles!

Shall we now continue to assert, in the world of the 1960's, that a State shall be permitted to mistreat U.S. citizens who live within its borders, simply because they are not white? Shall these States be free, as they once pleaded to be free in the staging of lynchings, to abridge or deny constitutional rights as though there were no U.S. Constitution? Shall they be permitted to continue "standing in the doorway," although everyone recognizes this as a mere exercise, albeit a vindictive one?

Shall the racially restrictive ordinance or the law of an illegally constituted lily-white city council or State legislature supersede the U.S. Constitution? Shall a police chief or a sheriff or a constable continue to be the arbiter of the rights of U.S. citizens?

One spokesman, the distinguished senior Senator from Georgia (and except in the human rights field he is distinguished), has declared the civil rights bill submitted to the Congress by President Kennedy to be "unpalatable." We submit that the daily diet of racial discrimination force-fed Negro citizens is the real "unpalatable" element in the present crisis. If the Senator from Georgia had to swallow our treatment for 24 hours, he would be on a picket line in the next following 20 minutes.

Contrary to a notion which some defenders of the racial status quo have advanced, the doings of the people on this issue are not subversive. On the contrary, they are thoroughly American. When Americans are stepped upon or pushed around, they protest and they demand corrective action.

Wherein is a demonstration against police brutality, against discrimination in employment, against exclusion from voting booths, lunch counters, and public recreation facilities judged to be un-American or subversive?

In truth, the resolute determination and action of our Negro citizens upon the civil rights issue constitute exemplary American conduct. If we desire to kill off such conduct and to fashion a nation of cautious crawlers, we should cease the teaching of American history.

It is no secret, that despite our military might and our industrial genius, our faltering fealty to the great ideal of "all men," set down in our Declaration of Independence, has shaken the confidence of the millions of mankind who seek freedom and peace. Do we mean "all men" or do we just say so? Is our Nation the leader of the free world or of the white world? Are we for democracy in southeast Asia, but for Jim Crow [name given to laws requiring segregation] at home?

Insofar as the Negro citizen and his allies renew and strengthen our fidelity to the founding purpose of our Nation, they put in their debt all those who maintain hope today, and all those who shall come after.

2

Kennedy's Civil Rights Proposal Is Not Strong Enough

John Lewis

While Congress considered President Kennedy's civil rights bill, three hundred thousand marched in Washington, D.C., in August 1963 to promote fair treatment for African Americans. The March on Washington is best remembered for Martin Luther King Jr.'s famous "I Have a Dream" speech. A lesser known oration delivered by twenty-three-year-old John Lewis, chairman of the Student Nonviolent Coordinating Committee (SNCC), caused the greatest behind-the-scenes controversy of the day. SNCC was a civil rights organization made up of fervent young activists. In preparing to represent the SNCC position, Lewis wrote a speech that criticized President Kennedy's proposed legislation and argued that a "nonviolent revolution" originating with the "masses" was "at hand." More conservative participants of the march who feared alienating the president and people in Congress demanded that the speech be modified. After much cajoling from march organizers and out of deference to a movement grandfather, A. Philip Randolph, Lewis toned the speech down. His original address capturing dissatisfaction with the bill is printed below.

From his teen years, John Lewis was active in the civil rights movement. Lewis organized lunch-counter sit-ins in Nashville, traveled on buses during the Freedom Rides, and led marchers across the Edmund Pettus Bridge in Selma, Alabama, on the infamous "Bloody Sunday." He served as chairman of SNCC from 1963 to 1966. Today, John Lewis repre-

John Lewis, with Michael D'Orso, *Walking with the Wind: A Memoir of the Movement*. New York: Simon & Schuster, 1998. Copyright © 1998 by John Lewis. Reproduced by permission of the publisher.

sents Georgia's fifth district in the House of Representatives, where he has served for nine terms.

W e march today for jobs and freedom, but we have nothing to be proud of, for hundreds and thousands of our brothers are not here. They have no money for their transportation, for they are receiving starvation wages, or no wages at all.

Problems with the Proposed Bill

In good conscience, we cannot support wholeheartedly the administration's civil rights bill, for it is too little and too late. There's not one thing in the bill that will protect our people from police brutality.

This bill will not protect young children and old women from police dogs and fire hoses, for engaging in peaceful demonstrations. This bill will not protect the citizens in Danville, Virginia, who must live in constant fear in a police state. This bill will not protect the hundreds of people who have been arrested on trumped-up charges. What about the three young men in Americus, Georgia, who face the death penalty for engaging in peaceful protest?

The voting section of this bill will not help thousands of black citizens who want to vote. It will not help the citizens of Mississippi, of Alabama and Georgia, who are qualified to vote but lack a sixth-grade education. "ONE MAN, ONE VOTE" is the African cry. It is ours, too. It must be ours.

> *We cannot support wholeheartedly the administration's civil rights bill, for it is too little and too late.*

People have been forced to leave their homes because they dared to exercise their right to register to vote. What is there in this bill to ensure the equality of a maid who earns $5 a week in the home of a family whose income is $100,000 a year?

For the first time in one hundred years this nation is being awakened to the fact that segregation is evil and that it must be destroyed in all forms. Your presence today proves that you have been aroused to the point of action.

We are now involved in a serious revolution. This nation is still a place of cheap political leaders who build their careers on immoral compromises and ally themselves with open forms of political, economic and social exploitation. What political leader here can stand up and say, "My party is the party of principles?" The party of Kennedy is also the party of [southern senator James O.] Eastland. The party of [moderate Republican senator Jacob] Javits is also the party of [conservative Republican senator Barry] Goldwater. Where is *our* party?

In some parts of the South we work in the fields from sunup to sundown for $12 a week. In Albany, Georgia, nine of our leaders have been indicted not by Dixiecrats [euphemism used for southern politicians] but by the federal government for peaceful protest. But what did the federal government do when Albany's deputy sheriff beat attorney C.B. King and left him half dead? What did the federal government do when local police officials kicked and assaulted the pregnant wife of Slater King, and she lost her baby?

The revolution is at hand, and we must free ourselves of the chains of political and economic slavery.

It seems to me that the Albany indictment is part of a conspiracy on the part of the federal government and local politicians in the interest of expediency.

I want to know, which side is the federal government on?

The revolution is at hand, and we must free ourselves of the chains of political and economic slavery. The nonviolent revolution is saying, "We will not wait for the courts to act, for we have been waiting for hundreds of years. We will not wait for the President, the Justice Department, nor Congress, but we will take matters into our own hands and create a source of power, outside of any national structure, that could and would assure us a victory."

A Time for Action

To those who have said, "Be patient and wait," we must say that "patience" is a dirty and nasty word. We cannot be patient, we do not want to be free gradually. We want our freedom, and we want it *now*. We cannot depend on any political party, for both the Democrats and the Republicans have betrayed the basic principles of the Declaration of Independence.

We all recognize the fact that if any radical social, political and economic changes are to take place in our society, the people, the masses, must bring them about. In the struggle, we must seek more than civil rights; we must work for the community of love, peace and true brotherhood. Our minds, souls and hearts cannot rest until freedom and justice exist for *all people*.

The black masses are on the march for jobs and freedom.

The revolution is a serious one. Mr. Kennedy is trying to take the revolution out of the streets and put it into the courts. Listen, Mr. Kennedy. Listen, Mr. Congressman. Listen, fellow citizens. The black masses are on the march for jobs and freedom, and we must say to the politicians that there won't be a "cooling-off" period.

All of us must get in the revolution. Get in and stay in the streets of every city, every village and every hamlet of this nation until true freedom comes, until the revolution is complete. In the Delta of Mississippi, in southwest Georgia, in Alabama, Harlem, Chicago, Detroit, Philadelphia and all over this nation, the black masses are on the march!

We won't stop now. All of the forces of Eastland, [southern politicians Ross] Barnett, [George] Wallace and [Strom] Thurmond won't stop this revolution. The time will come when we will not confine our marching to Washington. We will march through the South, through the heart of Dixie, the way [northern Civil War general William T.] Sherman did. We shall pursue our own "scorched earth" policy and burn Jim Crow to the ground—nonviolently. We shall fragment the South into a thousand pieces and put them back together in the image of democracy. We will make the action of the past few months look petty. And I say to you, WAKE UP AMERICA!

3

Support for the Civil Rights Law Is a Religious Obligation

Eugene Carson Blake

Bill sponsors actively sought the involvement of religious organizations. As Minnesota senator Hubert Humphrey stated: "The secret to passing the bill is the prayer groups." Humphrey was referring to a twenty-four-hour-a-day prayer vigil occurring at the Lincoln Memorial. Theology students from seventy-five seminaries kept the vigil going from April 19, 1964, until the law's passage. Backing from religious groups offered a moral edge to the proponents' arguments and also a means for reaching out to the rural Republican states in the west and midwest. Clergy from national religious organizations such as the National Council of Churches spoke to influential church members from states like Iowa and Nebraska who in turn lobbied their representatives in Congress.

Religious support was best exemplified by a massive rally that took place on April 28, 1964, at Georgetown University in Washington, D.C. Thousands of church leaders crammed the McDonough gymnasium to hear calls for the bill's passage. Speakers, who included Jewish, Protestant, Eastern Orthodox, and Catholic clergy, connected the civil rights cause to the ethical traditions of both Christianity and Judaism. The spirit of the evening is captured below by remarks made by Eugene Carson Blake, a Presbyterian minister, an international church leader, and a social activist.

In his speech, Reverend Blake uses theological justification to call for both change in the way blacks and whites interrelate and for passage of the civil rights bill. Specifically, the reality

Eugene Carson Blake, address at Georgetown University, Washington, DC, April 28, 1964.

that man is made in God's image places an obligation upon individuals to treat one another in a special manner. Discrimination against African Americans is a rejection of that obligation and a denial of that link between man and God. Blake then goes on to discuss how segregated schools and segregated public accommodations assault human dignity and are, hence, immoral. He speaks with anger about those who argue that integrating facilities denies rights of property to business people. Blake declares that Christians and Jews place the "rights of men" over the "rights of property."

Reverend Blake's address is entitled "Human Dignity—Have We Not All One Father?" It was placed in the *Congressional Record* by Senator Jacob Javits, a Republican supporter of the bill.

We are met here in Washington, representatives of the major religious institutions of this Nation, at a critical time in the life of the Nation and in the life of our churches and synagogues. We are in a contest, a long contest against those in our Nation who resist the new pattern of race relations which must be established if the United States of America is to survive as a citadel of freedom. . . .

The Theology of Civil Rights
Let me then remind you now of the unargued, and, I believe, unarguable morality upon which civil rights legislation and civil rights action is based. In our several traditions, the Judeo-Christian convictions about God and man are one in asserting:

> *Let me then remind you now of the . . . unarguable morality upon which civil rights legislation and civil rights action is based.*

1. That God made man in his image, which is to say that man is not merely an animal of a complicated sort but is in essence a spiritual being. His worth is not in his vigor, weight, or cleverness, but in his origin. Because man, every man, is created by God, he must be treated, despite his sin, as a potential son of God, by covenant between God and man.

2. Right relations among men is based upon a personal concern for each one which we believe is not only our concern but that of God himself.

3. The most important ethical considerations, and perhaps the only ones, are directly related to the effect of our actions upon the life and well-being of other men—all other men.

Because man, every man, is created by God, he must be treated . . . as a potential son of God, by covenant between God and man.

Look with me then at the aims of two sections of the civil rights legislation assigned to me, education and public accommodations, in the light of our spiritual and moral agreement. Of all the disabilities put upon minority peoples by our present patterns of segregation and discrimination, these two, in education and in the standing insults to human dignity, are clearly the most immoral in the terms I have just described morality.

The Immorality of Segregated Schools

What has long been known by educators and has 10 years ago been established by the courts is that education of pupils involuntarily segregated by race has such bad effects on the educational process itself that equal educational opportunity is in fact not available to the segregated minority. And I remind you that the educational effect is not much different when the segregated minority school is retained against the Constitution in a southern State or it's maintained by neighborhood racial ghettos in northern cities. The effect of this inequality of educational opportunity hurts boys and girls, produces teenage frustration, leading to crime and degeneracy. All of the learned discussions of the value of neighborhood schools is revealed to be quite irrelevant in the light of what segregated schooling is doing to some children of God. That the resolution of these problems will be difficult—North and South, all of us should know. That the problems must be solved and quickly in the name of God, let school boards and education commissioners remember. It will be costly. We must spend the money. But no religious man dare say that we do not have money or brains enough to do this job. . . .

Segregated Facilities and Human Indignity

Finally, as serious as offenses against opportunity for children, are offenses against the dignity of men. The legislation before the Congress with regard to public accommodations seems in one sense to be the least important title of the law. What good does it do a Negro to be accepted in a fine restaurant if he has a job so poorly paid he can't afford to eat out at all? How does being accepted in a motel fundamentally affect the life of any man? And white men ask, Don't Negroes really like to associate together? It is true that the right to vote, the opportunity for a good education, the chance at any job for which a man is qualified as well as promotion in the job by merit, and finally the opportunity to buy or rent a decent home in which to shelter and raise a family—all these seem of more fundamental and long-range importance than the right to eat a hot dog in a central city lunch counter. And yet, as far as morality is concerned, the right of human dignity is fully as important in race relations and perhaps even more important than all of these. Those of us who are white need to know what it does to a man's soul and spirit when he sees his wife insulted and his children's eyes beclouded when these senseless indignities are suffered, and he dare not protest for fear.

Where in the Holy Bible . . . can one find a single passage to support the rights of property as against the rights of men?

The argument against legislating a strong and universally enforcible public accommodations section to the bill is that such a law impairs the rights of business people to enjoy their property and to use it as they see fit. How can any Christian or Jew sit still when such an immoral argument is voiced? Where in the Holy Bible, in Old Testament or New, can one find a single passage to support the rights of property as against the rights of men? The only moral justification in our society for the rights of property is the protection it affords men against encroachment upon their freedom by other men or by Government. Have we learned nothing since the day Amos thundered against those who, for profit, degraded men? Have we become so enamored of things that we forget that we are men created by a just and loving God?

Let any man who wishes to use his property to serve the public and make his living by it, let any such man know now that he must serve all the public without discrimination. He may insist that his customers be clean. So be it. Any man can wash. He may require his customers to dress properly. So be it. In our affluent society even the poor can find a jacket or a dress to wear. He may require sobriety, quiet, orderliness and courtesy from those who wish his service. So be it. White people have no monopoly in any of them. But one thing he may not do and be a moral man—he cannot require a dark man to turn white or to enter by another door. This is an insult to another man, his brother by God's creation. No man may so use his property.

And unless we quickly understand what such standing insults in our society do to make peaceful men turn violent, and patient men lose their self control—we understand neither the first level of morals nor the depth of the crisis that race discrimination has brought to our once proud Nation.

Our task as churchmen is not to be expert in legislation or to tell the Congress how to legislate. But it is our task and it is our competence to cut through the fog of immorality that threatens every American home and every church and synagogue, and to say so that everyone can hear and heed— "Thus saith the Lord"—"Let justice roll down like waters and righteousness like an ever-flowing stream." "Woe to them who are at ease in Zion and to those who feel secure on the mountain of Samaria."

"Behold the days are coming saith the Lord God when I will send a famine on the land; not a famine of bread, nor a thirst for water, but of hearing the words of the Lord."

"He that hath ears to hear, let him hear."

4

The Civil Rights Act
Is the Result of
Mass Protest

Martin Luther King Jr.

Martin Luther King Jr. became a national figure in 1956 when
he and others led the Montgomery bus boycott. To keep the
momentum from the boycott going, protest organizers created
the Southern Christian Leadership Conference (SCLC). Dr.
King served as the president and main spokesperson for SCLC
and became, for many, the symbol of the civil rights movement. During the fifties and early sixties, SCLC and other
groups sponsored many actions including sit-ins, marches,
Freedom Rides and more. In 1963, SCLC led a series of dramatic marches in Birmingham, Alabama, a city considered at
the time to be the most segregated in the South. The Birmingham protests influenced President John F. Kennedy to
propose the legislation that would eventually become the Civil
Rights Act of 1964.

Throughout much of the sixties, King wrote "annual reports" on the status of the civil rights movement that appeared
in *The Nation*, a weekly magazine. In excerpts from two such
reports, printed below, King examines the relationship between the civil rights movement and the Civil Rights Act of
1964. In Part I, a report written before passage of the bill, King
discusses the power of nonviolent protest to change society
and cites the strong civil rights bill before Congress as evidence. Invoking the spirit of Birmingham, he challenges the
Senate to pass a tough bill. In Part II, King argues that demon-

Part I: Martin Luther King Jr., "Hammer of Civil Rights," *The Nation*, March 9,
1964, pp. 230–34. Copyright © 1964 by the Heirs to the Estate of Martin Luther
King Jr. Reproduced by permission of Writers House, Inc.
Part II: Martin Luther King Jr., "Let Justice Roll Down," *The Nation*, March 15,
1965, pp. 269–74. Copyright © 1965 by the Heirs to the Estate of Martin Luther
King Jr. Reproduced by permission of Writers House, Inc.

strations are a necessary part of the legislative process and identifies the Civil Rights Act of 1964 as an accomplishment of activists in the civil rights movement.

I

Exactly one hundred years after Abraham Lincoln wrote the Emancipation Proclamation [the 1863 document legally ending slavery in the South] for them, Negroes wrote their own document of freedom in their own way. In 1963, the civil rights movement coalesced around a technique for social change, nonviolent direct action. It elevated jobs and other economic issues to the summit, where earlier it had placed discrimination and suffrage. It thereby forged episodic social protest into the hammer of social revolution.

The Civil Rights Movement

Within a few months, more than 1,000 American cities and towns were shaken by street demonstrations, and more than 20,000 non-violent resistors went to jail. Nothing in the Negro's history, save the era of Reconstruction [period following the Civil War], equals in intensity, breadth and power this matchless upheaval. For weeks it held spellbound, not only this country, but the entire world. What had moved the nation's foundations was a genuinely new force in American life. Negro power had matured and was dynamically asserting itself.

The impact of this new strength, expressed on a new level, means among other things that the civil rights issue can never again be thrust into the background. There will not be "One hundred years of litigation," that cynical threat of the segregationists. Nor will there be easy compromises which divert and stagnate the movement. The problem will now be faced and solved or it will without pause torment and agonize the political and social life of the nation.

In the past two decades, the contemporary world entered a new era characterized by multifaceted struggles for human rights. Continents erupted under the pressures of a billion people pressing in from the past to enter modern society. In nations of both the East and the West, long-established political and social structures were fissured and changed. The issues of human rights and individual freedom challenged forms of government as dissimilar as those of the Soviet Union, colonial Africa, Asia, Latin America and the United States.

The Negro freedom movement reflects this world upheaval within the United States. It is a component of a world era of change, and that is the source of its strength and durability. Against this background the civil rights issue confronts the 88th Congress and the Presidential campaign of 1964.

Pushing for Meaningful Legislation

Earlier civil rights legislation was cautiously and narrowly drawn, designed primarily to anticipate and avoid Negro protest. It had a double and contradictory objective: to limit change, and yet to muffle protest. The earlier legislation was conceived and debated under essentially calm conditions. The bill now pending in Congress is the child of a storm, the product of the most turbulent motion the nation has ever known in peacetime.

Congress has already recognized that this legislation is imbued with an urgency from which there is no easy escape. The new level of strength in the civil rights movement is expressed in plans it has already formulated to intervene in the Congressional deliberations at the critical and necessary points. It is more significantly expressed in plans to guarantee the bill's implementation when it is enacted. And reserve plans exist to exact political consequences if the bill is defeated or emasculated.

As had been foreseen, the bill survived intact in the House. It has now moved to the Senate, where a legislative confrontation reminiscent of Birmingham impends. Bull Connor [Police Commissioner in Birmingham, Alabama] became a weight too heavy for the conscience of Birmingham to bear. There are men in the Senate who now plan to perpetuate the injustices Bull Connor so ignobly defended. His weapons were the high-pressure hose, the club and the snarling dog; theirs is the filibuster. If America is as revolted by them as it was by Bull Connor, we shall emerge with a victory.

The keys to victory in Birmingham were the refusal to be intimidated; the indomitable spirit of Negroes to endure; their willingness to fill the jails; their ability to love their children—and take them by the hand into battle; to leave on

Martin Luther King Jr. challenged the Senate to pass a strong civil rights bill and advocated nonviolent protest for civil rights.

that battlefield six murdered Negro children, [including four young girls who were killed when a black church was bombed in Birmingham], to suffer the grief, and resist demoralization and provocation to violence.

Argument will inevitably be made that in the Senate cloture is the only weapon available to subdue the filibuster. And cloture requires that a two-thirds majority be mustered before a simple majority can legislate. In thirty-five years, the only time that cloture has been successfully invoked was against a fragile liberal group opposed by the Administration regulars and almost the entire Republican delegation. That is hardly a convincing precedent for the success of cloture in the present fight.

On the other hand, if proponents of the civil rights measure will adopt some of the burning spirit of this new period, they can match their tenacity with that of the filibusterers.

The Dixiecrats can be worn down by an endurance that surpasses theirs. What one group of men dedicated to a dying cause can do, another group, if they are as deeply committed to justice, should be able to do. When the Southern obstructionists find themselves at the end of their physical and moral resources, cloture may be employed gently to end their misery.

It is not too much to ask, 101 years after Emancipation, that Senators who must meet the challenge of the filibuster do so in the spirit of the heroes of Birmingham. They must avoid the temptation to compromise the bill as a means of ending the filibuster. They can use the Birmingham method by keeping the Senate in continuous session, by matching the ability of the segregationists to talk with their capacity to outlast them. Nonviolent action to resist can be practiced in the Senate as well as in the streets.

There could be no more fitting tribute to the children of Birmingham than to have the Senate for the first time in history bury a civil rights filibuster. The dead children cannot be restored, but living children can be given a life. The assassins who still walk the streets will still be unpunished, but at least they will be defeated.

The important point is that if the filibuster is not beaten by a will to wear it out, the Dixiecrats will be justified in believing that they face, not an implacable adversary, but merely a nagging opponent. Negroes are not going to be satisfied with half a loaf of the legislation now pending. The civil rights forces in the Senate will have to find the strength to win a full victory. Anything less will be regarded as a defeat in the context of today's political realities. . . .

II

Are demonstrations of any use, some ask, when resistance is so unyielding? Would the slower processes of legislation and law enforcement ultimately accomplish greater results more painlessly? Demonstrations, experience has shown, are part of the process of stimulating legislation and law enforcement. The federal government reacts to events more quickly when a situation of conflict cries out for its intervention. Beyond this, demonstrations have a creative effect on the social and psychological climate that is not matched by the legislative process. Those who have lived under the corrosive humiliation of daily intimidation are imbued by demonstrations with a sense of courage and dignity that strengthens their personalities. Through demonstrations, Negroes learn that unity and militance have more force than bullets. They find that the bruises of clubs, electric cattle prods and fists hurt less than the scars of submission. And segregationists learn from demonstrations that Negroes who have been taught to fear can also be taught to be fearless. Finally, the millions of Americans on the side lines learn that inhumanity wears an official badge and wields the power of law in large areas of the democratic nation of their pride. . . .

The Civil Rights Act of 1964 . . . is historic because its enactment was generated by a massive coalition of white and negro forces.

What did we accomplish in 1963–64 specifically and where will it take us?

The Civil Rights Act of 1964 is important even beyond its far-reaching provisions. It is historic because its enactment was generated by a massive coalition of white and Negro forces. Congress was aroused by them from a century of slumber to a legislative achievement of rare quality. These multitudinous sponsors to its enactment explain why sections of the Act were complied with so hastily even in some hard-core centers of the South. . . .

The Civil Rights Act was expected by many to suffer the fate of the Supreme Court decisions on school desegregation. In particular, it was thought that the issue of public accommodations would encounter massive defiance. But this pessimism overlooked a factor of supreme importance. The legislation was not a product of charity of white America for a supine black America, nor was it the result of enlightened leadership by the judiciary. This legislation was first written in the streets. The epic thrust of the millions of Negroes who demonstrated in 1963 in hundreds of cities won strong white allies to the cause. Together, they created a "coalition of conscience" which awoke a hitherto somnolent Congress. The legislation was polished and refined in the marble halls of Congress, but the vivid marks of its origins in the turmoil of mass meetings and marches were on it, and the vigor and momentum of its turbulent birth carried past the voting and insured substantial compliance.

5

The Legislation Takes Away Basic Rights

Eugene Butler

The following editorial originally appeared in the May 1964 issue of *Progressive Farmer* and was written by Eugene Butler, the magazine's editor in chief. Butler contends that the bill is unconstitutional because it will grant so much unwarranted power to the federal government that individuals will be denied fundamental rights and states will be reduced to mere "appendages" of the national government. He argues that though the bill's proponents might have good intentions, they are creating an evil situation.

Butler cites several parts of the proposed legislation to make his case. For example, advocates had claimed that Congress could pass legislation that outlawed discrimination in public accommodations because the Constitution grants Congress the right to regulate interstate trade. Butler counters that the founders put the interstate commerce phrase in the Constitution to allow Congress to regulate trade between states not to tell a businessperson who they must or must not serve. Moving into the area of states' rights, Butler asserts that the Constitution allows states to establish voter qualification. He maintains that this power would be taken away from states by the civil rights act. Overall, Butler's root fear is that by denying the Constitution the proposed bill will permit the federal government to gain excessive power.

E ver since the War Between the States settled beyond doubt the supremacy of the National Government,

Eugene Butler, "Civil Rights: A Bill Full of Civil Wrongs," *Progressive Farmer*, May 1964.

States' rights have been whittled away by legislative action and court decisions. Now comes the National Government with a misnamed package of bills called civil rights that still further erodes States' rights. By its flagrant intrusion of Government into the private lives of citizens, it makes a mockery of their constitutional rights.

National Power

The bill takes away from State governments many rights the Founding Fathers thought they had guaranteed under the Constitution. If it is passed and sustained by the Supreme Court, it will prove once and for all that the States have left no rights that the Federal Government is obligated to respect.

The bill would do these things:

It would take away from the States their constitutional right to set voters' qualifications. It would force the States to qualify automatically for voting any of their citizens with a sixth-grade education.

It would tell business people, including farmers, how they may use their property and whom they may hire and fire.

It would take tax money from the people of the States and then refuse to give back to them their fair share unless they buckled under to the Federal Government's ideas of social equality and civil rights.

The bill proposes to regulate public accommodations. But what it does is to control privately owned establishments that cater to the public. There is a vast difference. Recent Supreme Court decisions have already legally desegregated public accommodations such as trains, streetcars, parks, and schools. The new bill goes much further. It seeks to control the business life of hotel owners, theater owners, and store owners, denying them the right to use their private property as they see fit.

The Bill Is Unconstitutional

The authors of the bill seek constitutional authority to regulate private business through the 14th amendment [passed after the Civil War in order to grant citizenship rights to African Americans] to the Constitution and that part of article 1, section 8, known as the commerce clause.

The 14th—the tainted amendment that was never legally ratified—states that: "No State shall make or enforce any law which shall abridge the privileges and immunities of citizens of the United States nor shall any State deprive any person of life, liberty, or property, without due process of law; nor deny to any person within its jurisdiction the equal protection of laws."

There is not a word in the amendment that gives Congress authority to legislate against a private business. It was designed solely to prevent a State from passing discriminatory laws.

Realizing how little the 14th amendment supports their position, the authors of the public accommodation proposal sought help from the commerce clause of article 1, section 8. This clause gives Congress power "to regulate commerce with foreign nations, and among the several States, and with the Indian tribes."

It is difficult to read into this simple statement Federal authority to tell a storekeeper whom he must serve.

If it is passed . . . , it will prove once and for all that the States have left no rights that the federal government is obligated to respect.

It seems obvious that those who drafted the Constitution meant exactly what they said. They were granting Congress power to regulate commerce among the several States. Moreover, records of the Constitutional Convention and a knowledge of the times bear out this interpretation.

The public accommodations clause not only applies to persons traveling from State to State or establishments doing business in many States. It applies to establishments doing business entirely within a State, if a substantial portion of the goods they use or services they offer have at one time or another traveled from one State to another.

Over the years, this commerce clause has been used time and time again to take rights away from the States and give them to the Federal Government.

In discussing what part of commerce Congress has the power to regulate, Woodrow Wilson [twenty-eighth president of the United States] said:

"Clearly, any part of the actual movement of merchandise and persons from State to State. May it also regulate the conditions under which merchandise is produced which is presently to become the subject matter of interstate commerce?

"Clearly not, I should say. Back of the conditions of labor in the field and in the factory lie all the intimate matters of morals and of domestic and business relationships which have always been recognized as the undisputed field of State law.

It seems obvious that those who drafted the
Constitution meant exactly what they said.

"If the Federal power does not end with the regulation of actual movement of trade, it ends nowhere, and the line between State and Federal jurisdiction is obliterated."

Historically, Congress began first to regulate the carriers; that is, the railroads, that moved goods from one State to another. Then it broadened its powers to regulate the goods themselves. Eventually, it claimed to have power under this simple clause to regulate the conditions under which goods were manufactured. It did seem that when Congress set itself to regulate the wages, hours of overtime, and labor relations under which goods move in interstate commerce, it had tortured and twisted out of the commerce clause all the Federal power possible. But under this new bill, it attempts to use the commerce clause to open up an entirely new field of control. It would control a soda fountain, if its syrup moved across State lines. The next step would be to control doctors whose patients travel across State lines.

Hiring Practice and Voting

The bill provides for Federal regulation in hiring, firing, promoting, and handling employees of all businesses with as many as 25 employees. It would be unlawful to fail or refuse to hire or to discharge any individual because of his race, color, religion, and national origin. No "right" to be free from discrimination is anywhere stated in the Constitution save in the 14th amendment. And that amendment prohibits States, not individuals or businesses, from denying equal protection of the laws. Moreover, in no previous interpretation of the commerce clause were private employment practices considered to affect commerce. The personnel—the people—that work for a business often determine whether it makes a profit or fails. If Congress has the right to tell a business whom it can hire or fire, then by all that is fair and right, it should guarantee that business a profit.

The 15th amendment [passed after the Civil War to grant voting rights to African Americans] to the Constitution gives Congress the power to pass appropriate legislation to protect the right to vote from abridgment by reason of race or color. But this new civil rights legislation would give Congress the power to decide the qualifications of voters. Nowhere in the Constitution is Congress given this power.

It is said that in many localities, literacy tests [device used to unfairly deny African Americans the right to vote] are mere subterfuges under which people are not allowed to vote because of the color of their skin. We do not believe anyone should be disqualified from voting by reason of his color. We realize there are areas of the South in which Negroes are in a majority. In those areas, heavy block voting by Negroes could create serious problems. But there is no way around giving all qualified persons the right to vote.

And the sooner all areas of the South make up their minds to this fact and educate their Negroes to vote intelligently, the better off we shall be in the South.

Under the Constitution, any requirement for voting imposed by a State must apply equally to all comers. But those who would pass this new "civil rights" bill are confusing the abuse of a thing with the thing abused. It is one thing for Congress to pass legislation to require the even application of a literacy test to all persons desiring to vote. This is constitutional; it is right and proper. But it is something entirely different—and decidedly wrong—to take away from the States the right to decide what sort of literacy test is to be applied to all. If anything, we should raise, rather than lower, requirements for voting. A sixth-grade education is not enough. If there is any one cornerstone upon which good government is based, it is an informed public.

There are no doubt people who believe the civil rights bill serves a good purpose. They are sincere in believing that a person has a right to buy a meal here or to be lodged there. But they are not weighing the consequences. Good ends ought never to be sought by bad means. The civil rights bill is an evil means of seeking an evil end. If it passes, the States will be further reduced to nothing more than appendages to the Central Government and largely subject to its control.

6

George Wallace's Criticisms of the Bill Are Wrong

James E. Clayton and Robert E.L. Baker

As a candidate in the Democratic primaries of 1964, Governor George Wallace of Alabama spoke out against the proposed civil rights bill. This was no surprise. In January 1963, Governor Wallace ended his inaugural address with the now famous words: "Segregation now, segregation tomorrow, segregation forever." What did surprise most people, and scare some, was how many northern votes Wallace attained. In the Maryland, Indiana, and Wisconsin primaries, Governor Wallace won, respectively, 42 percent, 30 percent, and 34 percent of the Democratic votes. Proponents of the bill were fearful that such success was an indication of opposition to the civil rights law throughout the nation. They knew that they needed to respond to Wallace's attack.

In the following editorial appearing in the May 17, 1964, *Washington Post*, journalists James E. Clayton and Robert E.L. Baker reply point by point to what they see as distortions put forth by Wallace on the campaign trail. Their rebuttal seeks to quell fears that the bill will destroy the rights of individuals and the rights of states. For instance, they argue that, despite the governor's assertions, the public accommodations section of the bill does not forbid private clubs from maintaining a whites-only membership. In response to the charge whites will lose their jobs, the authors state that employers will not be permitted or required to fire whites and hire African Americans. And though Wallace had posited that owners of boarding houses would have to take in anyone seeking housing, Baker

James E. Clayton and Robert E.L. Baker, "Rights Bill Facts Versus Wallace Views—Many of Alabama's Criticisms Are Identical to Those of Other Foes of Measure," *Washington Post*, May 17, 1964.

and Clayton assert that the bill excludes small boarding houses and does not keep the owner of bigger establishments from evicting tenants for drunkenness or other such offenses.

___

Throughout his current campaign in Maryland, Alabama Governor George C. Wallace has spoken again and again about the civil rights bill now before the U.S. Senate.

Many of his comments are identical to those of other opponents of the legislation. Following is a comparison of some Wallace statements with the provisions of the bill:

Public Accommodation

Wallace: "There is virtually no aspect of business life which will not be affected by the public accommodations section of this bill. If you are engaged in any profession where you offer your personal services, you cannot refuse to serve anyone without fear of violating this act. If an establishment offers goods and services for sale, hire or use and is open to the public, then it is subject to Federal regulation."

Fact: Many businesses will not be affected by this section of the bill. The bill does bar discrimination by hotels, motels, boarding houses, restaurants and other eating places, gasoline stations, movie houses and other places of amusement. It applies to other businesses only if they are located physically on the premises of one of these or closely connected to it.

___

The bill does bar discrimination by hotels, motels, . . . restaurants, . . . gasoline stations, movie houses and other places of amusement.

___

Wallace: "Under the provisions of this section of the act, the lawyer, doctor, beautician, or barber, plumber, public secretary-stenographer would no longer be free to choose their clientele."

Fact: The bill does not apply to lawyers, doctors, barbers, plumbers, beauticians, public secretaries, and so on unless their offices are located in, and they primarily serve, customers of a hotel, motel, restaurant, amusement place or gasoline station.

Wallace: "Fraternal and social organizations, churches, religious organizations, the Masonic lodge, the Knights of Columbus and all similar organizations could be subjected to Federal control."

Fact: The bill says that the public accommodations section does not apply to a bona fide private club or other establishment not open to the public except when its facilities are made available to guests in hotels and motels, customers of gasoline stations, restaurants or lunch counters, or spectators and participants at amusement places. It is this exception that Wallace calls a "sleeper designed to destroy the privacy of private clubs." The legislative history of the act makes clear that this exemption is intended to mean, for example, that a private golf course is free to discriminate except that if it lets white guests of a hotel use the course it must also let Negro guests of that hotel play.

The proprietor is barred from rejecting a guest because of his race . . . but he is not barred from rejecting a guest because he is drunk.

Wallace: "There is a common belief that the public accommodations section is only applicable to interstate commerce. [Power for Congress to regulate interstate trade is granted in the Constitution.] This is absolutely untrue. Any person, firm or corporation who pays a business license to a State or other governmental body can be included."

Fact: Wallace is apparently talking about a proposal made and rejected almost a year ago. This section of the bill applies to the businesses listed above if they are in interstate commerce. It also applies if these businesses discriminate because they are required to do so by State or local laws or by the activities of State or local officials.

Wallace: "The classic example is the neighborhood boarding house. The business is usually in the owner's home. Under the provisions of the bill we discuss, any and all transients would have the unqualified right to invade the owners' home and obtain lodging."

Fact: A neighborhood boarding house is exempt from the act if it has less than six rooms and is in the proprietor's home. Even in boarding houses that are covered by the act, there is no unqualified right to lodging. The proprietor is barred from rejecting a guest because of his race or religion but he is not barred, for example, from rejecting a guest because he is drunk or because he has children.

Fair Employment

Wallace: "An employer can lose his right to hire whomever he might choose—this power being vested in a Federal inspector who, under an allegation of racial imbalance or religious imbalance, can establish a quota system whereby a certain percentage of a certain ethnic group must be employed as supervisors, skilled and common labor."

Fact: The employer does lose his right to hire only whites or only Negroes because the bill bars discrimination in hiring because of race, sex, or religion. The power of hiring, however, is not vested in a Federal official. If an employer discriminates, a Federal court can order him to stop it and punish him if he continues. The bill neither establishes nor permits a quota system. It bars an employer from hiring a man because he is a Negro in exactly the same way it bars him from refusing to hire a man because he is a Negro.

In its first year, the bill would apply only to firms with 100 or more employees. After 3 years, it would apply to all firms with more than 25 employees. It would never apply to smaller firms.

The bill neither establishes nor permits a quota system.

Wallace: "An old and qualified employee must be fired although his personal abilities are valued and his services constitute a major portion of the goodwill of his employer Union; seniority systems [privilege granted based on employees' greater years of service] will be abrogated under the unlimited power granted to Federal inspectors to regulate hiring, firing, promoting, and demoting."

Fact: The bill makes it illegal to hire, fire, promote, or demote on grounds of race, religion, or sex. The bill does not require an employer to fire anyone. Union seniority would not be affected but unions would be barred from denying membership on racial or religious grounds.

Wallace: "It will take white men's jobs and turn them over to Negroes."

Fact: The Justice Department says the bill would make it just as illegal to fire whites in order to hire Negroes as it would to fire Negroes in order to hire whites. The bill would not require an employer to create jobs for Negroes but it would bar him from refusing to hire qualified Negroes solely because of their race.

Wallace: The Federal Government would preempt the field and this act would wipe out State fair employment acts.

The bill would . . . bar [an employer] from refusing to hire qualified Negroes solely because of their race.

Fact: The bill specifically says it does not preempt the field. It would wipe out State laws only if they conflicted with it or were ineffective.

Education

Wallace: "The U.S. Commissioner of Education would be empowered to enter a school and transfer children from one school to another to accomplish either racial or religious balance. In other words, your child could be transferred across town in order to meet the Government's requirement that a Protestant child be admitted for the sake of assuring that there are exactly the same number of Protestants, Catholics, and Jewish children enrolled."

Fact: The Commissioner of Education would have no such power. The bill specifically bars Federal agencies from activities encouraging the assignment of students to public schools in order to overcome racial imbalance. Wallace gets around this clause by arguing that other sections of the bill bar schools from discriminating. But a leading court decision says that assigning students by race to end imbalance is just as unconstitutional as assigning students by race to maintain segregation.

Housing

Wallace: "Through a blackmail process of threatening the homeowner with cancellation of his loan, Federal agencies can destroy the homogeneous neighborhood and dictate who you shall sell your real estate to, who you shall rent a room to, who will be your lease tenant."

"It is a back-door, open-occupancy bill."

Fact: Housing loans are specifically not covered by the bill. Apparently, Wallace is referring to the President's housing order of last fall.

That order bars banks and developers that receive Federal guarantees on housing loans from discriminating against customers on racial grounds.

Nothing in the order stops an individual from selling his house to any other individual.

Voting

Wallace: "Under this act, the Attorney General of the United States could control an entire important voting area by making general allegations of discrimination without accompanying proof of truth."

Fact: The bill gives the Attorney General no new power over voting except to allow him to ask that three Federal judges rather than one judge hear voting cases. What Wallace is apparently talking about is a proposal made and rejected last fall.

Wallace: "All State laws defining voter qualifications will be immediately modified."

Fact: The bill would modify requirements for voting in Federal elections, not State elections, in some states. It bars a State from applying different standards to Negro and white registrants. It bars States from using minor errors as grounds for rejecting would-be voters. It says that if a State uses a literacy test, anyone with a sixth grade education is presumed to be literate. In States where voting qualifications are applied evenly to all persons, the bill would have little, if any, effect.

Federal Aid

Wallace: "Through the heavy hand of Federal financing, the farmer, the realtor, the industrialist, the developer, and all other facets of the free enterprise system will be regulated to a degree that it will almost necessitate an OK from Washington before any action at all is taken."

Fact: The bill affects the farmer, realtor, industrialist, and developer in two ways. If he employs more than 25 persons, he would be barred from discriminating in hiring, firing, promoting, etc. If he receives financial aid from the Federal Government, he would be barred from discriminating in any way.

Chapter 3

Assessing the Act's Passage and Legacy

1

The Act's Immediate Success

Rowland Evans and Robert Novak

During debate on the Civil Rights Act of 1964, opponents
predicted that massive police power would be needed to enforce the bill. In particular, many felt that Title II, which required an end to segregation in public accommodations such
as restaurants, motels, and movie houses, would be met with
stiff opposition in the southern states. Such resistance did not
occur. Instead, compliance with the new law was typical. Political columnists Rowland Evans and Robert Novak illustrate
such cooperation in a 1964 article about Birmingham, Alabama. They remind the readers that a little over a year earlier, police dogs had been used to intimidate protesters who
were marching for an end to the system of segregation that
had long dominated the social life of Birmingham. The reporters then describe Mayor Albert Boutwell's plan to imple-
ment the 1964 legislation. Their description includes images
of southerners quickly adjusting to a new era of relations between African American and white citizens. Evans and Novak
conclude that the success of the act in Birmingham proves
that federal legislation was indeed needed to prod Southerners to permit integration.

Evans and Novak were newspaper reporters who collabo-
ratively wrote the syndicated column "Inside Report" from
1963 to 1993 as well as books on several presidents.

P erhaps it is only Birmingham purging itself. This city,
whose violence and murder spawned the civil rights bill

Rowland Evans and Robert Novak, "Birmingham: 'Keeping Our Fingers Crossed,'"
New Republic, August 8, 1964, pp. 17–18. Copyright © 1964 by The New Republic,
Inc. Reproduced by permission.

last summer, is now the hopeful symbol of Southern compliance with the new Act. Compliance in moderate, progressive Atlanta would have been no surprise. In segregationist, tension-ridden Birmingham, it seems a miracle.

But there are no miracles today in the South, particularly not in this raw-boned, blue-collar steel town that sprouted out of Alabama's coal and iron ore deposits during the industrial revolution. The story of Birmingham's decision to accept, not to fight, the toughest civil rights law in history is the story of fastidious planning, dating back to last summer even before President Kennedy had finally decided to ask Congress to outlaw discrimination in public accommodations.

"We're still keeping our fingers crossed," William (Billy) Hamilton, a slight, chain-smoking political technician, told us the other day. Hamilton is executive secretary to Mayor Albert Boutwell. One source of possible trouble is the lurking figure of [segregationist] Governor George Wallace. Wallace has been ominously quiet about Birmingham's new life. He might still turn triumph into disaster.

Birmingham Integrates

One motel (which shall be nameless) was schizophrenic about the new law's public accommodations section. When other motels and hotels decided to admit Negroes the moment President Johnson signed the new law, it threatened to hold out. City officials pleaded with the manager:

"The choice of course is yours, but if you can't go along please resign from the motel association. It is vital when the association issues its announcement of compliance that it be unanimous."

Reluctantly, the hold-out went along. The hotel and motel association's July 3 [1964] announcement proclaimed to "the travelling public and the citizens of Birmingham" that compliance "will be observed by all members."

One place to view the new Birmingham is the Parliament House, a swank motel with plush lounges and elegant bars—and, of course, a lily-white clientele until now. At the Parliament House one day last week, two Negro young women chatted softly over their meal in the pleasant, sun-lit lunchroom, surrounded by whites. Across the lunchroom, a white-collar Negro, sportily dressed, ate alone. The scene was scarcely credible in a city that a year ago was dishonored by the snarl of police dogs, the arrogant presence of Wallace's state troopers and the bombing-murder of children.

In the heart of downtown Birmingham, Abe Slotnik's 20th Century Restaurant, where lawyers and bankers like to eat lunch, was all white on the day we stopped in. "No one's come in here," Slotnik said. "When they do, they'll be served just like you. I'm not fighting the government."

So far there has not been any trouble worthy to be dignified as an "incident." The closest to it came one evening in the formal dining room of the Parliament House. Two white couples got up and walked out when a party of nine Negroes walked in. The whites had ordered their meal and left without paying.

"We let them go," a Parliament House clerk explained. "The food hadn't gotten to their table. But it was foolish of them. They probably found the same thing at the next place."

The City Creates a Plan

What has happened in Birmingham the past few weeks is not the start of the biracial millenium. But as a case study of compliance with a law repellent to the majority, today's Birmingham story is as encouraging as last year's violence was frightening.

It starts with a document composed by Billy Hamilton at the instruction of the Mayor and the request of the Chamber of Commerce shortly after the Senate adopted cloture on the civil rights bill. Cloture ended the filibuster [method employed by U.S. Senators to block legislation through the use of nonstop speechmaking] and assured passage of a strong bill.

The story of Birmingham's decision to accept, not to fight, the toughest civil rights law in history is the story of fastidious planning.

Acting on orders from Mayor Boutwell, Hamilton had been in and out of Washington for weeks, conferring with top Administration officials and with Northern businessmen with extensive interests in the South. Beginning last summer these businessmen had been secretly helping the Kennedy-Johnson Administration prepare the way for the law.

Dated June 23, Hamilton's document has become a classic. Mayors and Chambers of Commerce all over the South have asked for it to help their own adjustment to the public accommodations section of the new law. It has three basic features:

First, it makes no effort to "sell" compliance to reluctant businessmen.

As a case study of compliance . . . , today's Birmingham story is as encouraging as last year's violence was frightening.

Second, it states flatly that "the real danger of disorder or disruption of business will lie in reaching no decision at all—in making no plans" to deal with the sweeping changes of the new law. The absence of plan, it adds, "will leave revolutionary elements free to operate on their own initiative—in effect, fill a vacuum."

Third, it pledges police protection to proprietors of restaurants, hotels, motels, lunch counters and other "public accommodations," whether they plan to comply with the law or resist it until tested in the courts.

This pledge of police protection by the city of Birmingham, working with the business community, was the foundation on which the city built its compliance program. The dynamics of the civil rights revolution, particularly in the South, have proved that a reliable police force under the direction of men committed to law enforcement is the big obstacle to rule of the mob.

Birmingham learned this from the violence that spread through its streets last year. But last year, for example, Birmingham's police department did not have much of a chance. On several occasions (once right after a truce had been reached with the Negro demonstrators) Wallace's state troopers rolled into Birmingham, clubbing and bullying, and pre-empted the city's own law enforcement.

The drafting of the city document (labelled ponderously "An Informational Memorandum with Regard to the Civil Rights Act of 1964") followed a series of quiet discussions between city officials and half-a-dozen leading citizens of Birmingham, all of them members of the Chamber of Commerce. These meetings started in early May. Frank Newton, the president of the Chamber, and Crawford Johnson III, the president-elect carried the main load for business.

Mayor Boutwell, M.E. Wiggins, president of the city council, and Hamilton represented the city. From New York came Julius Manger, head of the Manger Hotel chain with headquarters at the Vanderbilt Hotel.

Southern Businesspeople Cooperate

Manger was one of a dozen Northern executives with business interests throughout the South who were summoned by President Kennedy to the White House last summer. They were asked to help prepare a new psychological climate among Southern businessmen and their traditional methods of dealing with the race question. For a year, they worked with Presidents Kennedy and Johnson and Attorney General Robert Kennedy and his deputies. They toured the South, not trying to sell the new civil rights bill but acting as mediators between Washington and Southern business, and between Southern business and Negro leaders.

When Boutwell called the first Birmingham meeting in May, it was as secret as a council of war. He told Birmingham business that once the law was signed, the city had to have a plan and that this plan had to be "announced to the world."

"We're not asking any of you to tell us whether you are or are not going to comply," the Mayor said. "We're simply informing you that there is no longer any doubt that the law is going through and that it will definitely include a public accommodations section. We must have a plan."

The pledge of police protection by the city of Birmingham . . . was the foundation on which the city built its compliance program.

A day or two before President Johnson signed the bill, the "informational memorandum" was sent to every member of the Chamber of Commerce, to all the newspapers (including Negro journals), radio and television stations. It got a lukewarm endorsement from the Negro press. The 13-page memorandum contained a detailed description of the public accommodations section, what enterprises would be exempt, and how the conciliation service would operate. It emphasized that Birmingham had "no statute, resolution, ordinance or other provision" for enforcement of the new law, but that once an entrepreneur had decided what to do—whether comply or resist—he would be fully protected by local police. By July 2, the day President Johnson signed the law, every establishment covered by the law had informed Mayor Boutwell of its willingness to comply.

The Plan Is Tested

What the city hoped was that responsible Negroes would test the restaurants, motion picture houses and hotels immediately, before rabble-rousers could whip up emotions either among Birmingham's Negroes or angry whites. This is precisely what happened.

On the evening of July 2, the Rev. Fred Shuttlesworth, leader of the city's Negroes, assembled his followers at Fifth Avenue and 16th Street. It was time to test the new law, he said. He advised his people to be ready for "massive resistance." He set Friday as the day for testing.

Instead of "massive resistance," Shuttlesworth's men quietly entered the Parliament House and were immediately taken to the dining room. They entered all the city's movie theaters and were ushered politely to seats. They entered Brittling's Cafeterias and were shown to the end of the line. They were accepted everywhere. Shuttlesworth was dumbfounded when the Negro testers reported back to him that not once had they been refused service.

As we write this, nothing has disturbed the tranquillity of desegregation in Birmingham. The extraordinary demonstration vindicates those who predicted last summer that desegregation in the Deep South was possible only if backed by the force of federal law. Only then would the moderates (who had always been willing to desegregate) be able to do so. Only then would the segregationists who had cried "never here" be able to save face.

There is a great lesson in Birmingham. Over the years, public figures from Dwight Eisenhower to [senator and 1964 Republican candidate for president] Barry Goldwater have said that progress in civil rights depends on a change in men's hearts, not new laws. Birmingham today seems to prove otherwise, that new laws are what make progress possible.

2

Who Were the Heroes?
What Was the Impact?

Robert D. Loevy

In the final chapter to his book on the Civil Rights Act of 1964, portions of which are printed below, political scientist Robert D. Loevy answers three important questions. What were the most important factors leading to passage of the bill? What impact did the law have? What lessons were learned from the odyssey of the Civil Rights Act?

In discussing the act's journey, Loevy concludes that politicians played the leading role. Specifically, Loevy views Everett Dirksen's decision to support the bill as pivotal for ending the filibuster that in turn led to the law's approval. As Republican minority leader, Dirksen's advocacy swung essential votes. Loevy then goes on to consider the impact of the two presidents, Johnson and Kennedy. He argues that Kennedy would have succeeded in pushing Congress to pass a civil rights bill but not one as strong as the bill Johnson obtained.

Loevy also examines the effect of the bill in three areas. He argues that the act ended the segregation of public accommodations quickly in the South, improved job opportunities for all minorities and women, and terminated legally sanctioned segregation in public schools. Loevy closes by citing important lessons learned from the country's experience debating and passing the law.

Robert D. Loevy has been a professor of political science at Colorado College in Colorado Springs since 1968. From 1963 to 1964, Loevy served in the office of Thomas H. Kuchel, Republican floor manager for the Civil Rights Act of

Robert D. Loevy, *To End All Segregation: The Politics of the Passage of the Civil Rights Act of 1964*. Lanham, MD: University Press of America, 1990. Copyright © 1990 by University Press of America, Inc. Reproduced by permission.

1964. He has written many books on the political process including two on the Civil Rights Act of 1964.

In his speech closing the Senate debate on the Civil Rights Act of 1964, Senator Everett Dirksen of Illinois used the terms "tedious" and "inexorable." These two words provided an apt description of the legislative history of the Civil Rights Act of 1964, from the moment when President Kennedy presented the civil rights bill to the Congress in June 1963 until the signing of the bill into law by President Johnson in July 1964. Throughout the entire period of congressional consideration of the bill, the Southerners made the process tedious through their many attempts at delay and dilution. On the other hand, supporters of the bill were able to keep the bill moving (even though at times that movement seemed almost imperceptible) toward inexorable final passage.

The Senate filibuster was the ultimate example of the tedium created as the bill moved toward enactment. The Senate debate set many records which lasted into the 1990s and which, because of subsequent changes in Senate rules of procedure, could possibly stand forever. The Senate debate lasted a total of 83 days. It consumed more than 6,300 pages in the *Congressional Record*. One estimate held that over 10 million words were spoken, with at least 1 million more words spoken during the earlier House debate on the bill. The 4 months Senate debate also set a record of 166 quorum calls and 121 roll call votes. . . .

Dirksen the Key

The fact that Everett Dirksen was the key to the cloture vote and final passage of the civil rights bill is perhaps the major conclusion to be drawn from any study of the Civil Rights Act of 1964. As early as 29 June 1963, less than three weeks after President Kennedy had sent the administration civil rights bill to Congress, Deputy Attorney General Nicholas Katzenbach wrote a memo to Attorney General Robert Kennedy pointing out that "we have to work out some tentative strategy" designed to get Dirksen to support the bill. Katzenbach went on to say that the Kennedy administration could not hope to get the bill through the

House of Representatives until they could convince House members they had a reasonable chance of getting Dirksen's support in the Senate. Although the memo did not say it specifically, the implication was that the House members all knew that Dirksen was the key to Senate passage of the bill and would not support civil rights in the House until they were reasonably convinced Dirksen could be persuaded to support the bill in the Senate. . . .

Can one man have so much power over the legislative process in a large nation?

Thus it appears that Dirksen was the ultimate target of the pro–civil rights forces from the very moment President Kennedy sent his civil rights bill to Congress. Even the emergency meetings at the White House in October 1963, ostensibly designed to win the support of [William] Mc-Culloch and [Charles A.] Halleck in the House of Representatives, were aimed, through McCulloch and Halleck, at Dirksen. Can one man have so much power over the legislative process in a large nation that his vote and support have to be sought from the very beginning of the legislative process? That is apparently what happened with Everett M. Dirksen and the Civil Rights Act of 1964. . . .

Who Was the Hero?

Who was the hero in the successful passage of the Civil Rights Act of 1964? Was it Martin Luther King, Jr., who completely changed the atmosphere on Capitol Hill where civil rights was concerned with his nonviolent demonstrations in Birmingham? Was it Nicholas Katzenbach, the deputy attorney general who served as top legislative strategist for both the Kennedy and Johnson administrations and who, from the very beginning, orchestrated every move of the bill so as to eventually end up with Dirksen's support? Was it Clarence Mitchell, Jr., and Joseph Rauh, Jr., the lobbyists for the Leadership Conference on Civil Rights who, for more than a year, put unrelenting pressure on all concerned for as strong a civil rights bill as possible? Was it William McCulloch of Ohio, the House Republican who pressed both Everett Dirksen and the Senate Democratic leadership to make sure that the strong House passed civil rights bill was not significantly weakened in the Senate? Was it Hubert Humphrey, the Democratic whip [party leader in Congress who organizes fellow party members] in the Senate, who did the final persuading and negotiating with Dirksen and, with his "great man hook," tried to catch Dirksen and haul him into the civil rights boat? Or was the hero Everett M. Dirksen himself, the man who had carefully and effectively organized his small band of Republican supporters in the Senate so that, at key moments in the legislative process, he had the final say on exactly what did and did not become law?

Everett Dirksen was so powerful that he had a choice in the matter.

No matter which of these men is cast as the ultimate hero, one fact remains clear. Everett Dirksen was so powerful that he had a choice in the matter, but King, Katzenbach, McCulloch, and Humphrey had little choice but to do what Dirksen wanted. Dirksen could have decided to support the civil rights bill, and it would have passed, or he could have decided not to support the civil rights bill, and it would have failed. No such all-powerful choices existed for King, Katzenbach, Mitchell and Rauh, McCulloch, and Humphrey. They wanted the bill passed, and therefore their only choice was to get Dirksen's support and, in the end, give him whatever he demanded in return for his support. King, Katzenbach, Mitchell and Rauh, McCulloch, and Humphrey were fortunate that, in the end, Dirksen did not demand as much as he might have for delivering the key votes for cloture.

Who Could Have Achieved a Stronger Bill— Kennedy or Johnson?

Many persons involved with the successful passage of the Civil Rights Act of 1964 commented on the question of whether President Kennedy, had he not been assassinated, could have delivered as strong a civil rights bill as President Johnson did. One of Lyndon Johnson's biographers [Merle Miller] put the point this way:

> The greatest difference between the 1964 civil rights bill as it would probably have been passed in that year

under Lyndon was that Lyndon made sure he got everything he asked for. Kennedy, faced with inevitable Senate opposition, would almost surely have compromised somewhere, traded the deletion of one section, say, for the passage of the rest. Lyndon refused to delete, refused to compromise, anywhere.

Robert C. Weaver, a leading black official in the Johnson administration, saw Johnson as both more committed and more skillful than Kennedy in getting a civil rights bill through Congress. Weaver said:

> I think Kennedy had an intellectual commitment for civil rights and a broad view of social legislation. Johnson had a gut commitment for changing the entire social fabric of this country. . . . I don't think we would ever have got the civil rights legislation we did without Johnson. I don't think Kennedy could have done it. He would have gone for it, but he was a lot more cautious than Johnson. . . .

Apparently Georgia Senator Richard Russell, the leader of the filibustering Southerners, was another person who saw the rise of Lyndon Johnson to the presidency as critical to the passage of such a strong civil rights bill. Clarence Mitchell, Jr., told a pro–civil rights Senate aide that he had a "frank discussion" with Senator Russell. The aide put Mitchell's report in his notes:

> As Mitchell reports this discussion, Russell also knows the jig is just about up. The main distinction which Russell drew between the situation now and the situation when President Kennedy was alive was that they [the Southerners] have absolutely no hope of ultimately defeating President Johnson on the bill itself or even gaining any major compromises or capitulations from President Johnson. Interestingly enough, Senator Russell stated that he felt they could have gained major compromises from Kennedy.

The general consensus seemed to be that President Kennedy probably would have obtained some sort of civil rights bill from Congress in 1964, but that it would not have been anywhere near as strong a bill as Lyndon Johnson obtained. It is sad to have to say it, but a large number of those involved with the Civil Rights Act of 1964 believed that the tragic assassination of President Kennedy helped the final passage of the bill by putting Lyndon Johnson in the White House.

I don't think we would ever have got the civil rights legislation we did without Johnson.

In retrospect, therefore, John F. Kennedy and Lyndon B. Johnson appear to have had something of a symbiotic political relationship (in the sense that each needed something important from the other). With his great speaking ability and his talent for inspiring political followers, John F. Kennedy convinced many Americans of the great need to pass civil rights legislation. Kennedy apparently lacked, however, the ability to get Congress to pass such legislation in a strong enough form to please strong civil rights supporters. Lyndon Johnson, on the other hand, lacked Kennedy's speaking ability and inspirational quality, but he had great talents for getting definite action on Capitol Hill. It might be said of the two men that, in terms of civil rights, President Lyndon Johnson was able to deliver on the exciting goals and promises so inspirationally presented by President John F. Kennedy. . . .

The Gettysburg of the Second Civil War

Throughout the debate on the Civil Rights Act of 1964, the Southern Democrats made many references to the Civil War and the fact that, in their opinion, the civil rights bill literally called for a "reinvasion" of the South by U.S. Government officials and a new period of vindictive "Reconstruction [period following the Civil War]." Although the comparison runs the risk of being overdrawn, the civil rights movement of the early 1960s can be described somewhat aptly as a second Civil War. The white violence against black demonstrators at Birmingham was the equivalent of the Southern attack on Fort Sumter. The "Irrepressible Conflict" of the 1860s had, by 1963, become the "Irrepressible Debate."

Clearly the Civil Rights Act of 1964 was the Gettysburg of this second Civil War. The entire structure of Southern segregation was based on keeping the United States Government from interfering in the "Southern way of life," and the key to keeping the United States Government out of the South had always been the filibuster weapon in the United States Senate. As a result, final passage of the Civil Rights Act of 1964 was nowhere near as important as the breaching of the filibuster citadel by the successful cloture vote. The cloture vote freed the Senate to act on civil rights, which in turn freed the entire Congress to act on civil rights, which in turn freed the United States Government to enter the South and put an end to most legal and governmental forms of racial segregation. . . .

Impact

Despite the frequent claims by the Southern Democrats that the public accommodations section of the civil rights bill was unconstitutional, equal access to public accommodations and every other major section of the bill were quickly declared constitutional when tested in court and appealed to the United States Supreme Court. Within five months of final passage of the Civil Rights Act of 1964, the Supreme Court ruled in *Heart of Atlanta Motel v. United States* that the commerce clause of the Constitution gave the Congress all the power it needed to integrate public accommodations, even when the wrong being corrected was "moral and social" rather than "economic." In something of a surprise move, the high court applied the law not only to restaurants and motels whose customers came mainly from out of state but also to restaurants and motels that received a substantial portion of their food and supplies from out of state.

Once the constitutional issue had been disposed of by the Supreme Court, the implementation of equal access to public accommodations throughout the American South went very smoothly. As pro-civil rights supporters had argued all along, racial integration of restaurants and motels was easily implemented by "voluntary compliance" once it was the law of the land and no restauranteur or motel owner had to fear losing customers to a competitor who was still segregated. The primary impact of the successful passage of the Civil Rights Act of 1964, therefore, was that virtually overnight black Americans could and did receive services in innumerable places of public accommodation that had previously been unavailable to them. The South's "peculiar institution" of racial segregation in public places disappeared almost immediately once the filibuster weapon was bested and Congress was free to end the "peculiar institution."

After equal access to public accommodations, clearly the most important part of the Civil Rights Act of 1964 was the provision calling for the cutting off of U.S. Government funds to state and local governments and institutions that practiced racial discrimination. As predicted, the desire for (if not the dependence on) U.S. Government dollars led all but the most reactionary governments and institutions to rapidly desegregate their facilities and the administration of their services. Congress subsequently became quite enamored of the funds "cutoff" as a tool for enforcing compliance with Congressional law, including it in several subsequent pieces of legislation (such as laws guaranteeing access to public facilities for the physically handicapped).

The primary impact . . . was that virtually overnight black Americans could and did receive services in . . . places . . . that had previously been unavailable to them.

The equal employment opportunity provision of the law that was so strongly supported by the AFL-CIO [American Federation of Labor–Congress of Industrial Organizations, a major labor union] had a significant impact on hiring practices in the United States and on the composition of the American work force. The law was used to gain wider access to equal employment opportunity for all minority groups, not just blacks, and was particularly effective in gaining greater employment opportunities for women. When combined with the funds "cutoff" provision, the EEOC [Equal Employment Opportunity Commission, established by the act to monitor compliance with mandate to end job discrimination] caused an immediate, dramatic, and visible increase in the number of minority and women workers in United States factories and offices.

By giving the United States Government strong powers to enforce school desegregation in the United States, the Civil Rights Act of 1964 brought about the quick demise of all forms of legal (de jure) school segregation. The law did not, however, bring an end to racially segregated schools caused by the existence of all black and all white neighborhoods (de facto segregation). The Congress attempted to further address this problem of segregated neighborhoods producing segregated schools in the Housing Rights Act of 1968, but the problem of de facto segregation continued to be a controversial one, particularly when United States courts began ordering the busing of students to schools in different neighborhoods in order to achieve integration.

Whether the voting rights provisions of the Civil Rights Act of 1964 were effective or not is a moot point. Within little more than one year after the passage of the 1964 act, Congress passed the Voting Rights Act of 1965 and included in it virtually all of the strong provisions which were suggested for the 1964 act but failed to be enacted. Clearly, the precedent of breaking a filibuster with a successful cloture vote was the great contribution of the Civil Rights Act of 1964 to voting rights. The major improvements in black voting participation in the American South that occurred in the late 1960s and early 1970s were the direct result of the 1965 act, not the 1964 act. . . .

Lessons for Other Peoples

The events leading to the introduction and passage of the Civil Rights Act of 1964 do provide some lessons for other peoples facing similar racial problems. One obvious lesson is the necessity for civil rights demonstrators to keep their protests defiant but *nonviolent*. As long as civil rights protests remained orderly and nonviolent, they built national support for the civil rights bill in Congress. When various protest groups turned to more violent demonstrations, some of them bordering on riots, support for civil rights reform was harmed rather than strengthened. . . .

Perhaps the most important lesson to be learned is the difficulty, in a democracy, of trying to exclude any major group from participating in the political process. Despite the great extent of racial segregation in the American South and the procedural barriers to reform established in the Congress, civil rights supporters still were able to harness the machinery of a representative democracy and enact a major civil rights bill. Once a society has extended democratic freedoms to one group of citizens, it can be argued it is only a matter of time until those democratic freedoms have to be extended to *all* citizens.

3

The Birmingham Protests Pushed President Kennedy to Act on Civil Rights

Adam Fairclough

In April and May of 1963, Martin Luther King Jr.'s Southern Christian Leadership Conference (SCLC) staged a series of demonstrations in the streets of Birmingham, Alabama. At the time, Birmingham was considered to be the most segregated city in the entire country. Local officials responded to the protests with a viciousness that shocked the nation and provoked worldwide sympathy for the marchers. Many protesters went to jail, including thousands of young people and King himself. The relentless pressure of mass arrests and images of official brutality projected throughout the globe ultimately led to a victory for SCLC. After Birmingham, leaders of the movement hoped to keep the momentum going. In August 1963, 250,000 people converged on Washington, D.C., in support of both the pending civil rights act and civil rights in general. Speeches given by leaders of the movement such as King and singers such as Joan Baez and Mahalia Jackson contributed to the peaceful and uplifting atmosphere.

What was the impact of these events? In the following selection, historian Adam Fairclough explores the question of how the 1963 demonstrations in Birmingham and the March on Washington affected the passage of the Civil Rights Act of 1964. Whereas some scholars emphasize the decisive role of politicians in bringing about the legislation, Fairclough concludes that the work of civil rights activists was more crucial to the law's enactment.

Adam Fairclough is a historian teaching at the University of East Anglia in Norwich, England. He has written several books on the civil rights movement.

D id the protests in Birmingham give birth to the civil rights bill, which Congress eventually enacted in 1964? SCLC [Southern Christian Leadership Conference, a civil rights organization], not unnaturally, believed so. "But for Birmingham," [Fred] Shuttlesworth [minister and local activist in Birmingham] boasted in 1964, "the Civil Rights Bill would not be before Congress today." Wyatt Walker [who organized action in Birmingham for SCLC] was even more emphatic: "Birmingham brought about the 1964 Civil Rights Act."

The Impact of Birmingham

The claim that Birmingham created the Civil Rights *Act* is difficult to sustain. The bill did not reach the statute book until July 1964, and until Lyndon Johnson became president it looked doubtful that it would pass at all. The assertion that Birmingham prompted the civil rights *bill*, on the other hand, is more plausible. The political scientist David Garrow, however, has challenged it. The Birmingham protests produced "no widespread national outcry," he argues, "no vocal reaction by the nation's clergy, and no immediate move by the administration to propose salutary legislation." Garrow suggests two reasons for this lukewarm response: the black rioting [a reaction to the bombing of Martin Luther King Jr.'s headquarters] of May 7 and May 12 [1963] which alienated white sympathy and confused the issue; and the absence of a single, clear goal that could be easily conveyed both to and by the press. Birmingham, he concludes, was far less effective than SCLC's campaign in Selma two years later, which led directly to the passage of the Voting Rights Act.

But this argument can be faulted on several grounds. Comparisons between Birmingham and Selma must be treated with caution. It is quite true, as Garrow notes, that Birmingham produced a relatively muted response from

Congress: Selma prompted nearly two hundred sympathetic speeches, Birmingham a mere seventeen. A simple statistical comparison, however, fails to reveal the fact that the political context of 1963 was very different from that of 1965. Non-Southern congressmen were far more wary about speaking out on civil rights in 1963. Most regarded it as a sure vote loser, and Northern Democrats were anxious to avoid a damaging intraparty dispute that would redound to the benefit of the Republican party. In 1965, with the Republicans routed in the previous year's elections, they felt less politically inhibited. By 1965, moreover, the nation had become more accustomed to the idea that the government ought to play a central role in combatting racial discrimination; far fewer people still maintained that the South's racial problems could be solved through local, voluntary action. Finally, by 1965 the civil rights movement had reached a higher stage of development; it enjoyed greater legitimacy and respectability.

President Kennedy and Birmingham

The success of Birmingham should not, in any case, be judged according to its impact on Congress: the initiative for the civil rights bill came from the administration, not the legislature. And the evidence strongly suggests that SCLC's demonstrations played a decisive role in persuading the Kennedy administration to introduce legislation. For two years Robert Kennedy [Attorney General and the president's brother] had attempted to deal with each racial crisis on an ad hoc basis. Birmingham finally convinced him that crises would recur with such frequency and magnitude that the federal government, unless it adopted a more radical policy, would be overwhelmed. Birmingham, Edwin Guthman [a press secretary] recalled, "convinced the President and Bob that stronger federal civil rights laws were needed. When [Burke] Marshall [in charge of the Justice Department's civil rights division] returned from Birmingham on May 17 . . . he flew with Bob to Asheville, North Carolina. . . . Aboard the plane they worked out the essential elements of the Civil Rights Bill." Five days later, the president confirmed that he was considering new legislation and that "the final decision should be made in the next few days." At the end of May, against the advice of most of his aides and cabinet officers, he decided to endorse his brother's strategy. Outlining the bill in his televised address of June 11, Kennedy noted that "the events in Birmingham and elsewhere have so increased the cries for equality that no city or state or legislative body can prudently choose to ignore them."

There was a direct connection, therefore, between SCLC's demonstrations and the introduction of the civil rights bill. Of course, the Kennedy administration had sponsored civil rights legislation before, only to see it fail in Congress. The difference now lay in the broad scope of the bill and, even more important, in the administration's determination to see the measure through Congress. Contemporaries agreed that Birmingham, and the protests that immediately followed it, transformed the political climate so that civil rights legislation became feasible; before, it had been impossible. Roy Wilkins of the NAACP refused to ascribe the civil rights bill to Birmingham alone: what happened before—the Freedom Rides, the integration crisis at the University of Mississippi, the legal battles over voter registration and school desegregation—had paved the

Civil rights demonstrators kneel in prayer outside a municipal building in Birmingham, Alabama.

ground and contributed to the political education of the Kennedys on civil rights. "I see the Birmingham episodes as clinching the business . . . [and] convincing the President at long last that we had to have legislation." Even allowing for such qualifications, history must regard Birmingham as the decisive factor. As Burke Marshall noted, "The Negro and his problems were still pretty much invisible to the country . . . until mass demonstrations of the Birmingham type."

SCLC's demonstrations played a decisive role in persuading the Kennedy administration to introduce legislation.

Why did Birmingham have such a profound impact on the administration's thinking? If direct action had died down after May 10, its effects would have been transient and indecisive. But the protests in Birmingham also sent shock waves across the South. The fact that white leaders had made concessions in a city notorious for its racial intransigence gave new hope to blacks in Baton Rouge, New Orleans, and other segregationist strongholds. Widely acclaimed as "the best-organized and most highly disciplined action ever mounted by Negroes," Birmingham became a model for SNCC [Student Nonviolent Coordinating Committee], CORE [Congress of Racial Equality], and local black movements. As James Farmer acknowledged, Birmingham showed the need to involve thousands rather than hundreds. "A score of Birminghams followed the first. Birmingham thus set the stage for a full-scale revolt against segregation." By the end of the summer the South had experienced about one thousand demonstrations involving more than twenty thousand arrests. Enthusiasm for direct action swept even the NAACP which, at its annual convention in July, called upon its local branches to employ "picketing, mass protest actions, [and] selective buying campaigns." As [historians August] Meier and [Elliott] Rudwick have written, Birmingham "both epitomized the change in mood and became a major stimulus for direct-action campaigns."

To the Kennedy administration, the growth of direct action represented a dangerous and disturbing development. Throughout the summer, the president warned against "demonstrations, parades and protests" that "create tensions and threaten violence and threaten lives." The civil rights bill was designed, in large part, to get blacks off the streets. It gave blacks a legal redress, thus obviating the need, in Kennedy's view, for "demonstrations which could lead to riots, demonstrations which could lead to bloodshed." The bill also proposed a professional, full-time federal mediation service, an idea which had been rejected at the time of the Albany protests. The improvised, "crisis-management" methods of the Justice Department no longer sufficed: the crises were too many and too dangerous. . . .

From Birmingham to Washington

The administration responded to pressure, King reasoned, not proposals. And in the aftermath of Birmingham he sensed that the time had come to escalate the pressure in order to achieve a decisive breakthrough. Blacks were aroused as never before, he told [Stanley] Levison and [Clarence] Jones [movement lawyers] on June 1; organized into a mass movement they could break the political logjam and convince the president to crusade for legislation. But the protests required a national focus, he added, such as a mass rally in Washington involving up to one hundred thousand people: "It would be a mass march and also a unified demonstration all over America." King's decisiveness made a deep impression upon the two advisers. The next day, discussing the conversation, they agreed that King's cautious and thoughtful nature made his sense of urgency all the more significant. The one thing he had learned about King, Levison observed, "is that Martin's assessment of how Negroes feel is a very acute one; that he doesn't go wrong on that." A week later, as SCLC began to canvass support for the idea of a March on Washington, Kennedy announced his intention to press for legislation. To King, the lesson was obvious. "When we started out in Birmingham, Alabama," he told his staff, "we didn't have one thing on paper—nothing." By creating the pressure for reform, however, "we got a Civil Rights Bill that had ten titles.". . .

The March on Washington

What did the march, for all its size, spectacle, and fervor, actually achieve? Very little, some argue. It is doubtful that it swayed many congressmen. Nor did it persuade the administration to change its strategy of postponing debate on the civil rights bill lest a prolonged filibuster bottle up the rest of its legislative program. Indeed, Kennedy was increasingly inclined to delay the decisive vote until after the 1964 elections. "This is going to be an eighteen-month delivery," he told the press on November 14. Looking back, Joseph Rauh [lobbyist for the bill] thought it "unreal to suggest that [the march] had anything to do with the passage of the Civil Rights Bill. Because three months later, when Kennedy was killed, the bill was absolutely bogged down." Had he lived, Kennedy would almost certainly have bargained part of it away—perhaps the crucial public accommodations section—in order to win Republican support. Many doubted that the bill would have passed in any shape. The impact of the march on the legislative process seems to have been minimal.

Yet the March on Washington did help the civil rights movement. Never before had leading representatives of the Catholic, Protestant, and Jewish faiths identified so closely and visibly with black demands. During the next ten months the churches proved to be the most effective champions of the civil rights bill, exerting an especially notable influence on congressmen from the Midwestern and Rocky Mountain states, where trade unions were generally weak and the black population relatively small. The religious leaders, Rauh admitted, "were troops that we had never had before. . . . It made all the difference in the world." As Norman Hill, one of the organizers, later argued, by involving the white churches the march helped "to generate an ongoing lobby" for the civil rights bill.

4

Affirmative Action Violates the Civil Rights Act

Allan C. Brownfeld

Though the Civil Rights Act of 1964 decisively changed many aspects of American life, it left other issues unresolved. Affirmative action, as it has become known, is one such issue. Title VII of the Civil Rights Act required an end to discrimination in job hiring against African Americans, other minorities, and women. This mandate generated many questions: If merely ending discrimination does not lead to the hiring of blacks and others, can employers work more aggressively to add minorities and women to the workforce? Can employers, for instance, give advantages to a prospective employee that is equally qualified to other candidates if he or she is African American? Can employers set aside a certain number of jobs in their workforce for African Americans? The aggressive hiring practices presented in these questions are commonly referred to collectively as affirmative action. The term is also applied when colleges actively recruit students of color and give them advantages in the acceptance process. Proponents of affirmative action argue that discrimination tends to be self-perpetuating, so active steps must be taken in order to fulfill the original intent of Title VII.

In the following article, Allan C. Brownfeld, a syndicated columnist, author, and speaker, outlines a position against affirmative action. He argues that programs which encourage hiring to specifically increase the number of minorities violate the original intent of the Civil Rights Act of 1964 and the spirit of the civil rights movement.

Discarding Racial Quotas in the Name of Fairness

Martin Luther King, Jr.'s dream of equal protection under the law is making a comeback in California and the courts.

The original American civil rights revolution sought to eliminate racial segregation and a host of race-based laws such as those which, in many states, made inter-racial marriage illegal. The goal of this movement was the creation of a genuinely "color-blind" society in which each person would be judged on individual merit rather than race.

When Congress passed the Civil Rights Act of 1964, its clear intent was to remove race as a consideration in the hiring of employees. Title VII was written to end discrimination in employment, and Section 703 (a) forbade any employer to "limit, segregate or classify his employees in any way which would deprive or tend to deprive any individual of employment opportunities or otherwise adversely affect his status as an employee because of such individual's race, color, religion, sex or national origin."

Even though the law was clear, some in Congress feared that it might be used in the future to foster a policy of reverse discrimination. Sen. Hubert Humphrey (D.-Minn.), one of the strongest supporters of this legislation, made it clear that, "Title VII does not require an employer to achieve any sort of racial balance in his work force by giving preferential treatment to any individual or group." In fact, Humphrey went so far as to promise on the Senate floor that he would physically eat the paper the bill was written on if it were ever used to require racial hiring preferences.

Civil Rights Act Forbids Quotas

Concerned about changing the old discrimination for a new form of bias, Congress made things clear in Section 703 (j) of Title VII: "Nothing contained in this title shall be interpreted to require any employer . . . to grant preferential treatment to any individual or to any group because of race, color, religion, sex, or national origin of such individual or group on account of an imbalance. . . ."

In the years since 1964, of course, this law has been violated repeatedly and affirmative action, racial quotas, minority set-asides [percentage of jobs set aside for African Americans in a particular business] and a host of other race-based programs have been initiated.

The civil rights movement no longer wanted an end to discrimination. Instead, it shifted gears and began promoting a different kind of discrimination. In his book, *Changing Course*, Clint Bolick notes that the NAACP [National Association for the Advancement of Colored People] and other civil rights groups quickly became revisionists and reversed the movement's goals of a "color-blind" society: "The revisionists purveyed a civil rights agenda in name only. The shift in focus was deceptively subtle, relying upon familiar terms with broad support, such as 'freedom' and 'equality.' In reality, however, the revisionists embarked upon an ambitious new program of social engineering and wealth redistribution that is profoundly antithetical to the traditional civil rights vision."

When Congress passed the Civil Rights Act of 1964, its clear intent was to remove race as a consideration in the hiring of employees.

Now, after years of reverse discrimination, a new civil rights movement is emerging to challenge the notion of group rights and race-based rewards. Consider some recent developments:

Four white students are suing the University of Texas Law School, claiming that its quota system for admitting blacks and Hispanics shut them out. "Plaintiffs are white and, for this reason, the law school evaluated their admissions applications under a different, higher standard than that applied to black and Mexican-American applicants," said Michael P. McDonald, counsel to the Washington-based Center for Individual Rights, who is representing the students. "As a result, the law school rejected the plaintiffs . . . while admitting less qualified and, in numerous instances, far less qualified, black and Mexican-American applicants."

Because of their skin color, "white," 5,000 applicants were prohibited from taking the firefighter exam in Los Angeles in February 1994. This injustice resulted from a 1974 consent decree between the city of Los Angeles and the Justice Department. The decree's interim and long-range goals effectively required the fire department to hire 50% of its firefighters from among minority groups.

A member of the Los Angeles Fire Commission, Michelle Eun Joo Park-Steel, declares that "Discrimination is against the fundamental values of American culture. It was wrong in the Jim Crow era [era of legally-mandated segregation] and it is wrong 100 years later. . . . The old policies of rigid goals are insensitive to current, legitimate needs of all citizens. Hostility toward any race is no longer acceptable. If Los Angeles is to become safer and more prosperous, it must establish a world-class attitude that gives everyone an equal opportunity to serve our city."

In May 1994, the three-judge panel of the 11th U.S. Circuit Court of Appeals unanimously found that the Birmingham (Alabama) Fire Department's promotion system illegally used harsh racial quotas in the name of eliminating past discrimination. In 1981, the city implemented a long-term goal of having blacks fill 28% of the positions in each city employment category. To reach that goal in the fire department, officials agreed that 50% of the firefighters promoted to the rank of lieutenant would be black. Raymond Fitzpatrick, Jr., an attorney for the white firefighters, said that the settlement resulted in blacks with low scores on promotion exams being unfairly moved ahead of higher-scoring white applicants. The 11th Circuit Court of Appeals agreed, saying the quota-based system violated both the 1964 Civil Rights Act and the Equal Protection Clause of the 14th Amendment.

A new civil rights movement is emerging to challenge the notion of group rights and race-based rewards.

In California, signatures are now being gathered to place the California Civil Rights Initiative on the ballot in 1996 [reference to California's Proposition 209, which passed in 1996]. It would amend the state constitution to read: "Neither the State of California nor any of its political subdivisions shall use race, sex, color, ethnicity or national origin as a criterion either for discriminating against or granting preferential treatment to any individual or group in the operation of the State's system of public employment, public education, or public contracting." This amendment would end quotas in college admissions and the awarding of public contracts.

America Lost Its Way on Civil Rights

Discussing the California initiative, two state senators, Quentin Kopp, an independent, and Bill Leonard, a Republican, note that "To many people, the U.S. has lost its way on civil rights. The ideals of the 1960s civil rights movement were unimpeachable: They exalted equal opportunity for everyone; a color-blind standard; and the fair treatment of people based on respect for their status as individuals, not as members of groups. Today, we have the opposite: quotas, reverse discrimination—indeed, a whole body of laws and regulations enforcing the entitlements of group rights."

Senators Kopp and Leonard declare, "That such a movement is necessary at all is a measure of just how badly skewed the notion of civil rights has become in this country. The initiative in California seeks merely to overturn racial and sexual discrimination—the original goal of the civil rights movement 30 years ago."

Martin Luther King, Jr., repeatedly argued that men and women should be judged "by the content of their character, not the color of their skin." It is unfortunate that we need a new civil rights movement to rekindle that vision and sad indeed that the old civil rights movement has become so comfortable with a form of discrimination from which it benefits. Fortunately, the belief in fair play, which still seems to motivate an overwhelming majority of Americans, gives every reason to believe that the new civil rights movement will succeed in reversing current negative trends toward racial division and polarization.

5

Affirmative Action: In the Tradition of the Civil Rights Act

Nicholas Lemann

In the following article, Nicholas Lemann advocates for affirmative action by tracing the historical course of the concept. He starts in 1961 with the origin of the term, moves into a discussion of the debate over the Civil Rights Act of 1964, and then describes how President Lyndon Johnson extended the meaning of the law through a speech given at Howard University in 1965. In that address, Johnson argued that the nation needed to go beyond "equality as a . . . theory" to "equality as a result," suggesting the necessity to do more than merely end discriminatory practice. Lemann feels that Johnson's call to more actively close the gap between whites and blacks logically led to affirmative action programs in both job hiring and in the college admissions process. Using the bill's history as a foundation, Lemann concludes by presenting arguments and data to explain why affirmative action is still needed.

Lemann contends that without affirmative action, the country would start to see fewer African Americans in jobs of all sorts. This would lead to subsequent drops in overall income for African Americans and an increased separation between black and white America. Overall, Lemann argues that affirmative action works, in that qualified African Americans attain consideration for jobs and colleges that they would not have received otherwise. In support, he cites a military plan for finding qualified African American generals, which allowed Colin Powell to become a military leader.

Nicholas Lemann, "Taking Affirmative Action Apart," *The New York Times*, June 11, 1995, pp. 36–43. Copyright © 1995 by *The New York Times*. Reproduced by permission.

Nicholas Lemann is currently a staff writer for *The New Yorker*. Previously, he edited the *Washington Monthly* and wrote for the *Atlantic Monthly* as well as other periodicals. He is the author of several books, including *Big Test: The Secret History of the American Meritocracy* and *The Promised Land: The Great Black Migration and How It Changed America*.

Compton is a mostly Black and Hispanic, down-at-the-heels, inner-ring suburb of Los Angeles known to the outside world mainly as the home of rap groups like N.W.A. (Niggas With Attitude—its first album was "Straight Outta Compton"). On a quiet blue-collar street of tract houses with lawns that need mowing stands, incongruously, a fancy new house with a BMW parked in its bricked front courtyard. There's a touch of Graceland about it, the poor boy's mansion. Inside the front door is a large, round marble-floored entrance foyer overlooked by a balcony. There is a swimming pool in the backyard.

The house belongs to Dr. Patrick Chavis, a 43-year-old obstetrician-gynecologist with an enormous practice comprising entirely poor people on Medicaid. Chavis is where he is because he was swept up in a historical tide. He is a beneficiary of affirmative action. In 1973, he and four other African-Americans were admitted, under a special minorities-only program, to the University of California Medical School at Davis. Although all of the five were good students, medical-school admission is extremely competitive and none would have been admitted purely on the basis of undergraduate records. They got in because they were black, and therefore took the places of five white applicants with better grades and test scores.

> *Simply abolishing the South's legal apartheid system—the thrust of the Civil Rights Act— wasn't going to solve America's racial problems.*

One of these was a young engineer named Allan Bakke. He sued the medical school for discriminating against him on the basis of his race. The case went to the Supreme Court, resulting in its best-known decision to date on affirmative action: In June 1978, Bakke was ordered admitted (he too is a doctor today) and the special program was abolished. The Court also ruled, however, that universities could make being a minority a plus factor in their admissions decisions. Bakke v. Regents of the University of California was, then, an endorsement of affirmative action, but an extremely limited one. In the years following the decision, U.C.-Davis medical school admitted fewer blacks. Post-Bakke, Patrick Chavis couldn't have become a poorfolks' doctor. . . .

Birth of a Concept

How did we get to this peculiar point? Whose idea was affirmative action in the first place? How did it spread? What does it actually consist of? And does it do any good? The affirmative action trail begins faintly at the time of the Presidential inauguration of John F. Kennedy.

"We seek . . . not just equality as a right and a theory but equality as a fact and equality as a result."

At the Texas State Society's inaugural ball, Lyndon Johnson, the incoming Vice President, was pressing flesh in the receiving line. When a young black lawyer from Detroit named Hobart Taylor Jr.—known to Johnson because Hobart Taylor Sr., a businessman in Houston and an active Democrat, was a close friend—came through the line, Johnson pulled him aside and said he needed something. An executive order banning discriminatory hiring by Federal contractors was being drafted for President Kennedy's signature; could Taylor help work on it?

The next day, Taylor holed up in a room at the Willard Hotel with two future Supreme Court Justices, Arthur Goldberg and Abe Fortas, to prepare a document with the not-very-catchy title of Executive Order 10925. "I put the word 'affirmative' in there at that time," Taylor later told an interviewer for the archives of the Lyndon Baines Johnson Library. "I was searching for something that would give a sense of positiveness to performance under that executive order, and I was torn between the words 'positive action' and the words 'affirmative action.' . . . And I took 'affirmative action' because it was alliterative."

The key point about the inception of affirmative action is that it went virtually unnoticed. Executive Order 10925 merged two obscure Eisenhower Administration committees that were supposed to prevent discriminatory hiring—one aimed at the civil service and the other at Federal contractors—under the name of the President's Committee on Equal Employment Opportunity. The committee met 12 times. Its main activity was a program called "Plans for Progress," in which big Federal contractors were persuaded to adopt voluntary efforts to increase their black employment.

Although the committee did not exercise much direct power and was not in the news, its basic mission clearly would offend present-day critics of affirmative action, since it was to promote race-conscious hiring. There wasn't any conservative backlash against the committee, because practically no one knew it existed. But as soon as President Kennedy proposed a civil rights bill in 1963, opponents began attacking it as one that would impose racial-quota hiring schemes [specific percentage or number of jobs set aside for African Americans]. During the titanic Congressional debate that followed Johnson's proposing the Civil Rights Act in 1964, quotas were a frequent theme. "The bill would discriminate against white people," said Senator James Eastland of Mississippi. ". . . I know what will happen if the bill is passed. I know what will happen if there is a choice between hiring a white man or hiring a Negro both having equal qualifications. I know who will get the job. It will not be the white man."

There would be an enormous decrease in black representation everywhere in white-collar (and also blue-collar) America.

The Civil Rights Act, therefore, contained a sentence explicitly disavowing quotas. And, although the law created an Equal Employment Opportunity Commission to prevent job discrimination, the commission was given no powers of enforcement whatsoever, so that it could not promote quota hiring; it was taking away the E.E.O.C.'s enforcement power that prevented a Senate filibuster against the bill and so made its passage possible.

The passage of the Civil Rights Act set in motion a series of events that ended with President Johnson's issuing what is now regarded as the originating document of affirmative action: Executive Order 11246. Bear in mind what was on the minds of liberals at that time. Simply abolishing the South's legal apartheid system—the thrust of the Civil Rights Act— wasn't going to solve America's racial problems. There were small urban race riots in the summers of 1963 and 1964 and a large one in Watts in 1965. The gap between black and white was shockingly large. At the time, blacks were almost twice as likely as whites to be poor, twice as likely to be unemployed and more than four times as likely to be illiterate. The voices warning against quotas and reverse discrimination all seemed to belong to Southern segregationists, like Senators Eastland, Sam Ervin of North Carolina, Lister Hill of Alabama, J. William Fulbright of Arkansas and John Tower of Texas. So the anti-quota argument looked like merely a cover for something less legitimate.

The Invisible Milestone

The fullest expression of the liberal mood was a commencement address that President Johnson gave at Howard University on June 4, 1965. The key phrase (supplied by the young Daniel Patrick Moynihan) was, "We seek . . . not just equality as a right and a theory but equality as a fact and equality as a result." "Equality of result" has long been used by the opponents of affirmative action as the perfect distillation of the principle they find odious, but Johnson's speech was regarded within the White House as a great political triumph and the phrase generated no objections from the public.

Affirmative action specifically, however—the originating document, Executive Order 11246, issued on September 24, 1965—appears to have been a kind of accident.

The Civil Rights Act made the President's Committee on Equal Employment Opportunity, traditionally headed by the Vice President, potentially irrelevant, because it created several new Government agencies to make sure blacks weren't being discriminated against. In February 1965, Johnson created a new President's Council on Equal Opportunity, to be headed by his vice president, Hubert Humphrey, a lifelong crusader for civil rights; this made Humphrey chairman of a White House committee and a

White House council on the same thing.

Johnson ordered Humphrey to come up with a reorganization plan for all the Government's civil rights organizations. Humphrey responded by proposing to abolish the equal opportunity committee but to keep alive the equal opportunity council. The council would be in charge of "community relations" (one of the new functions created by the Civil Rights Act) and of making sure Federal contractors didn't discriminate against black job applicants—that is, affirmative action.

On June 21, 1965, shortly after his speech at Howard, Johnson approved this plan of Humphrey's. As late as mid-August, it was still on track. Then, in September, Johnson changed his mind. The reason is unknown, but it may have had to do with Humphrey's having made a hard-charging black lawyer named Wiley Branton the director of the equal opportunity council, which raised the possibility of controversial and high-profile civil rights enforcement actions emanating from the White House. A memo from a White House lawyer to Johnson, dated September 20, 1965, lays out a scheme to abolish Humphrey's council entirely rather than give it more power. Community relations would be given to the Justice Department and affirmative action to a new Office of Federal Contract Compliance Programs in the Labor Department. . . .

Black America is still a substantially separate world.

The reason that Executive Order 11246 did, in fact, turn out to be a milestone is that it took affirmative action out of the White House, which is under intense perpetual scrutiny and has a small staff with high turnover, and made it the raison d'être of a division of the Labor Department. This meant there would be a much larger and more permanent staff devoted to carrying out affirmative action—a staff with the power to write Federal regulations and with the maneuvering room that comes from the press not reporting on your every move.

Because the end of segregation came in the form of a bill being passed, the country realized it was making a momentous change. The Civil Rights Act of 1964 was furiously debated and examined. Compromises were struck. The result was that by the time the act became law, Americans had consciously made up their minds to take this great step. Executive Order 11246 had exactly the opposite dynamic: it was an invisible milestone that was not debated at all (or noticed, even) before the fact. Given its significance, it was inevitable that it would be publicly debated with Civil Rights Act–like intensity at some point after the fact—and now we are at that point. . . .

The Case for Affirmative Action

What would the country look like without affirmative action? According to its opponents, a gentle notching downward would take place in black America: black students who now go to Harvard Law School would go to Michigan instead and do very well; black students at Michigan would go to Louisiana State, and so on. The net impact would be small. And maybe then we would get to work on the real issues, like the poor quality of many all-black urban public schools.

The other possibility is that there would be an enormous decrease in black representation everywhere in white-collar (and also blue-collar) America, with a big, noticeable depressive effect on black income, employment, homeownership and education levels. The percentage of blacks in managerial and technical jobs doubled during the affirmative action years. During the same period, as Andrew Hacker pointed out in his book "Two Nations," the number of black police officers rose from 24,000 to 64,000 and the number of black electricians from 14,000 to 43,000. If affirmative action were entirely abolished, does anyone really believe the Government would undertake, say, an expensive upgrade of education for blacks as a more meaningful substitute?

Black America is still a substantially separate world. Blacks are by far the most residentially segregated ethnic group and the least likely to intermarry. Without affirmative action, the gap would surely become even more pronounced. The lack of faith in the fairness of the system that is so much more a part of the black world than the white would only increase.

The goal of affirmative action is not to reject the spirit of integration in favor of race-consciousness but to bring blacks into the mainstream of national life. The ironic result of affirmative action being abolished could be an increase, not a decrease, in the kind of black demands for reparations and mandated percentages of the action that whites find so annoying: if you're out of the system completely, then you don't seek access to jobs and school places. You just want more resources.

The opponents tend to treat affirmative action as a unitary evil: all the many varieties are equally wrong and disastrous, and the most extreme Frank Washington-type excesses are a fair representation of the totality of the phenomenon. In fact, the country is full of affirmative-action plans that work pretty well and affirmative-action beneficiaries whom people like. Clifford Alexander, who was head of the Equal Employment Opportunity Commission, was Secretary of the Army in the Carter Administration; he says that the first time a list of people being promoted to general landed on his desk, he sent it back, demanding that more good black candidates be found. One of these was Colin Powell, who recently departed from his usual sphinx-like silence on public issues to make a speech defending affirmative action. In California, the psychic center of the affirmative-action debate is undergraduate admissions to Berkeley; the initiative literature uses the statistic that "the dropout rate for students admitted under affirmative-action programs often runs as high as 75 percent." According to the university, 60 percent of its black students (there are only about 200 in each class of 3,000, by the way) graduate within six years, as against 84 percent of white students. Rather than Berkeley cruelly taking its black students up past their "level," it has a black graduation rate 50 per cent higher than the national average. . . .

Every child born in America doesn't have access to good schools and doesn't have parents who encourage study. Many blacks go to the worst schools and live in the toughest family circumstances. To argue that by late adolescence black people have run a fair competitive race and that if they're behind whites on the educational standards they deserve to be permanently barred from the professional and managerial classes is absurd. It constitutes not just a denial of opportunity to individuals but a denial of talent to the society.

The Case of Dr. Chavis

Allan Bakke, after graduating from medical school, did his residency at the Mayo Clinic in Minnesota. Today he is an anesthesiologist in Rochester, Minn. Bakke doesn't speak to the press and he didn't respond to my request for an interview. He does not appear to have set the world on fire as a doctor. He has no private practice and works on an interim basis, rather than as a staff physician, at Olmsted Community Hospital.

Patrick Chavis, who took Allan Bakke's place at U.C.-Davis med school, fits the stereotype of the affirmative-action beneficiary in one way: as he freely admits, he would not have been admitted strictly on the basis of his grades and test scores, though they were good. In other ways, though, he does not fit. He is not a product of the cushy black upper class: he grew up in South Central Los Angeles, the eldest of five children of a welfare mother who had migrated to California from rural Arkansas. Chavis first met his father three years ago, when he was 40. One day when he was in high school, one of his teachers used the word "indigents" in class. That night, upset, he asked his mother if that word meant people like them. "Who else do you think it means?" she asked him.

Another way in which Patrick Chavis doesn't fit the stereotype of the affirmative-action beneficiary is that he doesn't give the impression of being tormented by self-doubt over whether he really deserves to be where he is. If anything, he seems to assume a superiority over his white medical-school classmates. He says he works harder than they do and in tougher conditions. He and his four black classmates set up a primary-care clinic when they were at Davis and worked there as volunteers, but they couldn't get any of the white students to join them. While he was still a resident at the University of Southern California, he and one of his black classmates from Davis each put up $500 and opened a small practice, so that they could "hit the ground running" when they graduated. He ticks off what the black doctors admitted under Davis's special minorities-only program (which was eliminated after the Supreme Court's Bakke decision, resulting in subsequent classes having only one or two black members) are doing now: almost all are in primary care in underserved areas, including his ex-wife, Toni Johnson Chavis, a pediatrician in Compton. If Chavis hadn't gotten into medical school, his patients wouldn't be treated by some better-qualified white obstetrician; they'd have no doctor at all and their babies would be delivered the way Chavis was—by whoever happened to be on duty at the emergency room of the county hospital. . . .

So Patrick Chavis fiercely defends affirmative action and holds himself up as an example of the good that it does. "There's no way in hell—if it wasn't for some kind of affirmative action, there wouldn't be any black doctors," he says. "Maybe one or two. Things haven't changed that much."

Appendix: Excerpts from the Civil Rights Act of 1964

Title II—Injunctive Relief Against Discrimination in Places of Public Accommodation

Sec. 201. (a) All persons shall be entitled to the full and equal enjoyment of the goods, services, facilities, and privileges, advantages, and accommodations of any place of public accommodation, as defined in this section, without discrimination or segregation on the ground of race, color, religion, or national origin.

(b) Each of the following establishments which serves the public is a place of public accommodation within the meaning of this title if its operations affect commerce, or if discrimination or segregation by it is supported by State action:

(1) any inn, hotel, motel, or other establishment which provides lodging to transient guests, other than an establishment located within a building which contains not more than five rooms for rent or hire and which is actually occupied by the proprietor of such establishment as his residence;

(2) any restaurant, cafeteria, lunchroom, lunch counter, soda fountain, or other facility principally engaged in selling food for consumption on the premises, including, but not limited to, any such facility located on the premises of any retail establishment; or any gasoline station;

(3) any motion picture house, theater, concert hall, sports arena, stadium or other place of exhibition or entertainment; and

(4) any establishment (A)(i) which is physically located within the premises of any establishment otherwise covered by this subsection, or (ii) within the premises of which is physically located any such covered establishment, and (B) which holds itself out as serving patrons of such covered establishment. . . .

Title VII—Equal Employment Opportunity

Discrimination Because of Race, Color, Religion, Sex, or National Origin

Sec. 703. (a) It shall be an unlawful employment practice for an employer—

(1) to fail or refuse to hire or to discharge any individual, or otherwise to discriminate against any individual with respect to his compensation, terms, conditions, or privileges of employment, because of such individual's race, color, religion, sex, or national origin; or

(2) to limit, segregate, or classify his employees or applicants for employment in any way which would deprive or tend to deprive any individual of employment opportunities or otherwise adversely affect his status as an employee, because of such individual's race, color, religion, sex, or national origin.

(b) It shall be an unlawful employment practice for an employment agency to fail or refuse to refer for employment, or otherwise to discriminate against, any individual because of his race, color, religion, sex, or national origin, or to classify or refer for employment any individual on the basis of his race, color, religion, sex, or national origin.

(c) It shall be an unlawful employment practice for a labor organization—

(1) to exclude or to expel from its membership, or otherwise to discriminate against, any individual because of his race, color, religion, sex, or national origin;

(2) to limit, segregate, or classify its membership or applicants for membership, or to classify or fail or refuse to refer for employment any individual, in any way which would deprive or tend to deprive any individual of employment opportunities, or would limit such employment opportunities or otherwise adversely affect his status as an employee or as an applicant for employment, because of such individual's race, color, religion, sex, or national origin; or

(3) to cause or attempt to cause an employer to discriminate against an individual in violation of this section.

Chronology

April 3–May 10, 1963
Under the direction of the Southern Christian Leadership Conference (SCLC) and Martin Luther King Jr., a nonviolent protest is launched against discrimination in Birmingham, Alabama, one of the most segregated cities in the country. The U.S. Justice Department plays an important role in bringing the SCLC and local Birmingham officials together for negotiations. Victory is ultimately achieved for the SCLC, but not before images of brutality against the demonstrators is broadcast throughout the country on television.

June 11, 1963
President John F. Kennedy goes on national television to call for major civil rights legislation.

June 12, 1963
Medgar Evers, NAACP field secretary in Mississippi, is assassinated in the driveway of his home just hours after President Kennedy's speech.

June 19, 1963
President Kennedy's Justice Department completes work on its version of acceptable civil rights legislation and sends it to Congress for consideration.

June 19–November 20, 1963
Because of stiff opposition expected in the Senate, President Kennedy's version of the civil rights law begins its journey in the House of Representatives. The bill is introduced first in Subcommittee Number 5 of the Senate Judiciary Committee. Emanuel Celler, a liberal Democrat, works with William M. McCulloch, a moderate Republican, to attain the committee's approval in late October. The bill is then sent on to the House Rules Committee.

August 28, 1963
More than 250,000 civil rights demonstrators assemble in Washington, D.C., demanding freedom and economic

justice. They also call for the passage of meaningful civil rights legislation. Despite expectations of violence by many, the gathering is peaceful. All events are televised to the nation, allowing Americans to hear Martin Luther King Jr. deliver his famous "I Have a Dream" speech.

September 15, 1963

The Sixteenth Street Baptist Church in Birmingham, the center for many of the demonstrations that took place the previous spring, is bombed. Four young girls in the basement of the church are killed.

November 22, 1963

President Kennedy is assassinated in Dallas, Texas. His vice president, Lyndon Johnson of Texas, becomes the thirty-sixth president of the United States.

November 27, 1963

President Johnson addresses the entire Congress and calls for "the earliest passage of the civil rights bill" as an "honor to President Kennedy's memory."

January 9–30, 1964

The bill meets stiff opposition in the House Rules Committee by its chair, Howard W. Smith of Virginia. After pressure from colleagues, the committee votes to move the proposed bill on to the floor of the House.

February 1964

Senate Democratic leaders appoint Senator Hubert H. Humphrey of Minnesota as floor manager for the legislation. He quickly organizes a bipartisan team with Republican minority whip Thomas Kuchel to work for the bill's passage. Included on the team are civil rights lobbyists Clarence Mitchell and Joseph Rauh of the Leadership Conference on Civil Rights.

February 9, 1964

In an attempt to kill the proposed legislation, Representative Smith asks that the word "sex" be added in the sections of the bill that relate to job discrimination. His amendment is accepted.

February 10, 1964

After nine days of debate, the House of Representatives approves the proposed civil rights legislation. The vote is

290 to 130 with 138 of the yea votes coming from Republicans.

March 1964

The Senate begins formal consideration of the pending civil rights legislation.

March–June 1964

Southern senators begin a filibuster, which continues throughout the Senate's consideration of the bill.

April 1964

CBS News places newscaster Roger Mudd on the steps of Congress for continuous reporting of progress concerning the civil rights bill.

April 19–June 19, 1964

On April 19 students from seventy-five seminaries (Protestant, Catholic, and Jewish) begin a round-the-clock prayer vigil at the Lincoln Memorial in support of the civil rights bill. They stay until the bill is passed in the Senate.

April 28, 1964

An interreligious rally is held at Georgetown University in Washington, D.C., by church leaders of all major faiths. Thousands are in attendance.

June 10, 1964

Republican senator Everett Dirksen rises on the floor of the Senate and calls for an end to the filibuster and passage of the civil rights bill. The Senate ends the filibuster with a vote of 71 to 29. Given that it takes two-thirds of the Senate to end a filibuster, proponents had only four more votes than they needed to move the bill forward.

June 19, 1964

The Senate passes the bill by a 73 to 27 vote.

July 2, 1964

After the House formally approves the Senate version of the bill, it is signed by President Johnson during a ceremony at the White House. The signing is preceded by a televised speech delivered by Johnson. From the White House, he tells the nation that the bill's purpose is "to promote a more abiding commitment to freedom" and the heart of the bill will come to be "because most Americans are law-abiding citizens." In attendance at the speech and signing are legislators central to the bill's passage, such as Hubert Humphrey, and civil rights leaders, such as Martin Luther King Jr.

March 17–August 6, 1965

Congress passes and President Johnson signs the Voting Rights Act of 1965. The act strengthens voting provisions in the Civil Rights Act and leads to a new era of African American political involvement.

June 4, 1965

President Johnson delivers a speech at Howard University where he speaks about the Civil Rights Act of 1964 and calls for "equality of result." This phrase initiates what becomes known as affirmative action, a more aggressive approach to ending forms of discrimination addressed by the Civil Rights Act of 1964.

For Further Research

Books

Irving Bernstein, *Promises Kept: John F. Kennedy's New Frontier*. New York: Oxford University Press, 1991.

Taylor Branch, *Parting the Waters: America in the King Years, 1954–1963*. New York: Simon and Schuster, 1988.

———, *Pillar of Fire: America in the King Years, 1963–1965*. New York: Simon and Schuster, 1998.

Carl M. Brauer, *John F. Kennedy and the Second Reconstruction*. New York: Columbia University Press, 1977.

William H. Chafe, Raymond Gavins, and Robert Korstad, eds., *Remembering Jim Crow: African Americans Tell About Life in the Segregated South*. New York: New Press, 2001.

Adam Fairclough, *To Redeem the Soul of America: The Southern Christian Leadership Conference and Martin Luther King Jr.* Athens: University of Georgia Press, 1987.

David J. Garrow, *Bearing the Cross: Martin Luther King Jr. and the Southern Christian Leadership Conference*. New York: William Morrow, 1986.

Hugh Davis Graham, *The Civil Rights Era: Origins and Development of National Policy, 1960–1972*. New York: Oxford University Press, 1990.

Bernard Grofman, ed., *Legacies of the 1964 Civil Rights Act*. Charlottesville: University Press of Virginia, 2000.

Byron C. Hulsey, *Everett Dirksen and His Presidents: How a Senate Giant Shaped American Politics*. Lawrence: University Press of Kansas, 2000.

Robert D. Loevy, *To End All Segregation: The Politics of the Passage of the Civil Rights Act of 1964*. Lanham, MD: University Press of America, 1990.

———, ed., *The Civil Rights Act of 1964: The Passage of the Law That Ended Racial Segregation*. Albany: State University of New York Press, 1997.

Robert Mann, *The Walls of Jericho: Lyndon Johnson, Hubert Humphrey, Richard Russell, and the Struggle for Civil Rights.* New York: Harcourt Brace, 1996.

Edward L. Schapsmeier and Frederick H. Schapsmeier, *Dirksen of Illinois: Senatorial Statesman.* Urbana: University of Illinois Press, 1985.

Carl Solberg, *Hubert Humphrey: A Biography.* New York: W.W. Norton, 1984.

Mark Stern, *Calculating Visions: Kennedy, Johnson, and Civil Rights.* New Brunswick, NJ: Rutgers University Press, 1992.

Timothy Nels Thurber, *The Politics of Equality: Hubert H. Humphrey and the African American Freedom Struggle.* New York: Columbia University Press, 1999.

Denton L. Watson, *Lion in the Lobby: Clarence Mitchell Jr.'s Struggle for the Passage of Civil Rights Laws.* New York: William Morrow, 1990.

Robert Weisbrot, *Freedom Bound: A History of America's Civil Rights Movement.* New York: W.W. Norton, 1990.

Charles Whalen and Barbara Whalen, *The Longest Debate: A Legislative History of the 1964 Civil Rights Act.* Cabin John, MD: Seven Locks Press, 1985.

Richard Wormser, *The Rise and Fall of Jim Crow.* New York: St. Martin's Press, 2003.

Periodicals

Alexander M. Bickel, "The Civil Rights Act of 1964," *Commentary*, August 1964.

———, "Much More than Law Is Needed," *New York Times Magazine*, August 9, 1964.

John H. Johnson, ed., "Special Report: Twenty-Five Years After the Civil Rights Act of 1964, What's Changed, What Hasn't?" *Ebony*, August 1989.

N.T.N. Robinson III, ed., "The Controversy over the 'Equal Employment Opportunity' Provisions of the Civil Rights Bill," *Congressional Digest*, March 1964.

———, "The Controversy over the 'Public Accommodations' Provisions of the Kennedy Civil Rights Proposals," *Congressional Digest*, November 1963.

Philip M. Stern, "An Unexpected Dividend for the South," *Harper's*, May 1965.

U.S. News & World Report, "What Editors in the South Say Now: Interviews on the Outlook for Race Relations," June 29, 1964.

———, "With New Civil Rights Law—How Negroes See the Future," June 29, 1964.

Pat Watters, "The South Learns to Live with the Civil Rights Law," *Reporter*, August 13, 1964.

Websites

Civil Rights Project, Harvard University, www. civilrightsproject.harvard.edu. This site stems from a project devoted to studying issues confronted during the time of the civil rights movement but not yet resolved. The site includes links to civil rights organizations and news about contemporary civil rights issues.

CongressLink, www.congresslink.org. CongressLink is a "nonprofit, nonpartisan research and educational organization" sponsored by the Dirksen Congressional Center. The site provides both contemporary and historical information about the U.S. Congress.

John F. Kennedy Library and Museum, www.cs.umb.edu/jfklibrary. This website, connected to the JFK Library and Museum in Boston, contains documents related to the Kennedy presidency, including press conferences, speeches, letters, and more. The site also includes biographical information about John F. Kennedy.

Lyndon Baines Johnson Library and Museum, www.lbjlib. utexas.edu. This website, connected to the LBJ Library and Museum in Austin, Texas, contains a multitude of documents related to the Johnson presidency, including oral histories of people associated with the Johnson administration, speeches, daily diaries, photos, and more. It also includes information about the life and presidency of Lyndon Baines Johnson.

Index